ADAPT
AND
THRIVE

Historical Principles of Resilience and Reinvention

FELIX GRAYSON

MINDSPARK
PUBLISHING

To those who dare to grow, adapt, and reinvent themselves—this book is for you.
May your journey be one of courage, discovery, and endless possibility.

"Life isn't about finding yourself. Life is about creating yourself."

— *George Bernard Shaw*

ABOUT STONED PHILOSOPHER

Welcome to the *Stoned Philosopher* series—where timeless wisdom meets the modern world.

Each book distills powerful lessons from history's greatest minds, leaders, and thinkers—transforming their ideas into practical insights for today's challenges.

From mastering habits, calm, and resilience to understanding success, leadership, and meaning, this collection invites you to think deeper, live wiser, and see life from new perspectives.

Whether you're exploring *Modern Zen*, uncovering *The Wisdom of Warriors*, or seeking clarity through *The Art of Perspective*, every title offers a journey toward self-mastery and understanding.

Discover the full *Stoned Philosopher* collection and more at **FelixGrayson.com**, home of **Mind-Spark Publishing**—where knowledge, philosophy, and storytelling come together to spark lifelong curiosity.

Wisdom isn't something we find—it's something we grow into.

Let the journey begin.

CONTENTS

INTRODUCTION: THE COURAGE TO REINVENT

Life is a canvas of constant change. At times, it sweeps us up in waves of transformation, pushing us toward uncharted territories. At other times, it challenges us to pause, reflect, and make deliberate choices about who we are and who we wish to become. This book is an invitation to embrace that journey—a journey of reinvention.

Reinvention is more than adaptation; it is an act of creation. It requires courage, curiosity, and resilience. It asks us to reimagine our identities, release what no longer serves us, and step boldly into the unknown. While the process can feel daunting, it is also profoundly liberating, offering us the chance to align with our true values, unlock new possibilities, and thrive in the face of uncertainty.

This book explores the art and practice of reinvention through the lens of history, philosophy, and contemporary innovation. It draws on timeless wisdom and modern insights to provide a roadmap for navigating change, building resilience, and seizing opportunities in an ever-evolving world.

A World in Flux

We live in a time of unprecedented transformation. Technological advancements are reshaping industries and societies at a breakneck pace. Global interconnectedness has created new opportunities for collaboration, yet it has also introduced complexities that demand agility and innovation. Social and cultural shifts are redefining norms, challenging us to rethink what it means to lead meaningful and fulfilling lives.

In such a world, reinvention is not optional—it is essential. Whether we are navigating personal transitions, professional shifts, or broader societal changes, the ability to adapt and evolve has become one of the most valuable skills of our time.

Yet, reinvention is not merely a response to external forces. It is also a deeply personal act of growth and self-discovery. It requires us to confront our fears, question our assumptions, and embrace the potential within ourselves. In doing so, we not only navigate change but also shape it, creating lives and legacies that reflect our highest aspirations.

The Heart of Reinvention

At its core, reinvention is about perspective. It is the ability to see challenges not as insurmountable obstacles but as opportunities for growth. It is about recognizing that failure is not the opposite of success but a stepping stone toward it. It is about cultivating the mindset, skills, and strategies needed to navigate uncertainty with confidence and purpose.

This book is organized around these themes, weaving together historical examples, philosophical reflections, and actionable insights to illuminate the path of reinvention. From the stoic wisdom of Marcus Aurelius to the bold innovations of Elon Musk, from the resilience of Mahatma Gandhi to the adaptability of modern entrepreneurs, these stories remind us that reinvention is both timeless and universal.

The lessons of reinvention are not confined to extraordinary individuals—they are accessible to all of us. They invite us to reflect on our own lives and ask: What do I need to let go of to move forward? What possibilities are waiting to be explored? How can I align my actions with my values to create a life of meaning and impact?

Why This Book Matters Now

The need for reinvention has never been more urgent. As we face a rapidly changing world, many of us find ourselves at crossroads—personally, professionally, or collectively. We may be grappling with questions about our careers, our relationships, or our purpose. We may be navigating the aftermath of disruption, seeking stability, or striving to break free from old patterns.

This book is a guide for those moments. It offers tools and insights to help you embrace change, build resilience, and move forward with clarity and confidence. Whether you are embarking on a new chapter, confronting unexpected challenges, or simply seeking to grow, the principles of reinvention will empower you to navigate the journey with courage and creativity.

The Invitation to Begin

Reinvention begins with a choice—the choice to step into the unknown and trust in your ability to create something new. It is not a journey that requires perfection, but one that thrives on curiosity, persistence, and openness.

In the pages ahead, you will find stories of individuals who have transformed themselves and the world around them. You will explore practical strategies for reframing challenges, building emotional strength, and taking purposeful action. You will uncover the tools needed to let go of the past, adapt to the present, and shape the future.

This book is more than a guide—it is an invitation. An invitation to dream bigger, to take risks, and to trust in your capacity to grow. It is a reminder that reinvention is not reserved for moments of crisis but is a lifelong practice that allows us to evolve and thrive.

The Journey Awaits

As you embark on this journey, know that you are not alone. The stories and insights within these pages are a testament to the shared human experience of growth and transformation. They remind us that reinvention is not a solitary act but one that connects us to a greater whole—a world of possibility, creativity, and progress.

Each chapter of this book is a step along the path of reinvention, offering inspiration, guidance, and practical tools to help you navigate change with confidence and purpose. As you read, reflect on how these lessons resonate with your own journey and consider how you can apply them to the challenges and opportunities in your life.

Reinvention is a journey of courage, creativity, and discovery. It is a testament to the resilience of the human spirit and the limitless potential within each of us. As you turn the page and begin this exploration, I invite you to embrace the art of reinvention—to step into the unknown, to grow, and to create a life that reflects your highest vision.

The journey begins now. Let's take the first step together.

CHAPTER 1: THE POWER OF PERSPECTIVE – REFRAMING CHALLENGES

The Role of Mindset in Adversity

Adversity is an inevitable part of life. Its arrival is often unpredictable, and its presence can feel insurmountable. Yet, throughout history, one truth has remained constant: it is not the challenge itself but the way we perceive and respond to it that determines our ability to endure and thrive. This profound insight underscores the power of mindset in shaping our relationship with hardship, a theme echoed in the writings of great thinkers like Marcus Aurelius and Viktor Frankl, who turned unimaginable adversity into sources of strength and wisdom.

Stoicism: Marcus Aurelius and the Mastery of Mindset

Imagine ruling an empire under constant siege — plagued by war, political treachery, and disease. For Marcus Aurelius, Roman Emperor and stoic philosopher, this was daily life. Despite such immense burdens, Aurelius's enduring wisdom wasn't born from his circumstances but from his response to them. His personal journal, later compiled into *Meditations*, reveals a profound philosophy centered on the idea that external events lie beyond our control, but our perceptions of them are entirely within our power.

Aurelius taught that adversity is not inherently good or bad—it is our judgment that labels it as such. By mastering our thoughts, we can transcend the chaos of external events. He wrote, "You have power over your mind—not outside events. Realize this, and you will find strength." For Aurelius, challenges were not curses but opportunities to practice virtues like patience, resilience, and courage.

In the face of hardship, adopting a stoic mindset means asking, *What can this situation teach me?* Instead of succumbing to frustration or despair, we can focus on what lies within our control: our actions, thoughts, and attitudes. By doing so, we free ourselves from the grip of external chaos, channeling energy into meaningful and constructive responses.

Viktor Frankl: Finding Meaning in the Midst of Suffering

Centuries later, another thinker would expand on this idea under the most harrowing conditions imaginable. Viktor Frankl, an Austrian neurologist and psychiatrist, endured years of unimaginable suffering in Nazi concentration camps. Stripped of his freedom, his family, and his dignity, Frankl faced an existence defined by profound loss and cruelty. Yet within this darkness, he found a guiding light: the conviction that life's meaning is not dictated by circumstance but by one's internal search for purpose.

In his groundbreaking work, *Man's Search for Meaning*, Frankl reflected on how those who survived the camps often shared a common trait: the ability to find meaning in their suffering. He famously wrote, "Everything can be taken from a man but one thing: the last of the human freedoms—to choose one's attitude in any given set of circumstances, to choose one's own way."

Frankl's insight reveals a powerful truth: while we may not control the adversities we face, we retain the ultimate freedom to decide how we interpret and respond to them. This perspective shifts adversity from an oppressive force to a transformative one, allowing individuals to extract meaning from even the bleakest experiences. Frankl himself attributed his survival to his focus on reuniting with his wife and the hope of finishing his work on logotherapy—a psychological approach centered on finding meaning as a pathway to healing.

The Science of Mindset: Modern Validation of Ancient Wisdom

While the teachings of Aurelius and Frankl are rooted in philosophical reflection and personal experience, modern psychology provides scientific validation for the transformative power of mindset. Studies on resilience reveal that individuals with a growth mindset—who view challenges as opportunities for learning and development—are significantly more likely to thrive under stress. This perspective aligns with what psychologists call cognitive reappraisal: the process of reinterpreting a negative event in a way that reduces its emotional impact.

For instance, research into post-traumatic growth highlights how individuals who frame adversity as a catalyst for personal growth often emerge from hardship with greater strength, empathy, and wisdom. This does not diminish the pain of adversity but emphasizes the potential for transformation that lies within it. The key lies in the stories we tell ourselves about our struggles and our ability to redefine those narratives.

Applying the Lessons: Building a Resilient Mindset

So how can we cultivate a mindset that empowers us to face adversity? The first step is awareness—recognizing the role of our thoughts in shaping our experiences. When confronted with a challenge, pause and reflect: *What story am I telling myself about this situation? Is there a different way to see it?* This simple act of mindfulness can interrupt the spiral of negativity, opening the door to a more constructive response.

The next step is intentional practice. Just as physical strength requires consistent training, mental resilience grows through deliberate effort. Practices like journaling, meditation, and gratitude exercises can help rewire our thought patterns, fostering a mindset of strength and adaptability. By focusing on what we can learn rather than what we have lost, we begin to see adversity not as an obstacle but as an opportunity.

Lastly, draw inspiration from the wisdom of those who have walked this path before. The stoicism of Marcus Aurelius and the meaning-centered philosophy of Viktor Frankl remind us that while adversity is inevitable, suffering is not. Our power lies in our response—a truth that transforms hardship into a proving ground for our inner strength.

By shaping how we view and respond to adversity, our mindset becomes our greatest ally. It enables us to find clarity amid chaos, purpose in pain, and ultimately, strength in the face of life's challenges. This is the power of perspective— the ability to reframe hardship not as a roadblock but as a bridge to growth and resilience.

Seeing Opportunity in Difficulty

Adversity often arrives uninvited, disrupting plans and casting uncertainty over our lives. Yet, for those who choose to embrace it, difficulty can become fertile ground for growth, innovation, and success. The ability to see opportunity in hardship is not an innate gift but a cultivated skill—a skill that has transformed failures into triumphs and ordinary individuals into extraordinary visionaries. By reframing challenges as stepping stones, we unlock the potential for reinvention and discovery that lies hidden within every setback.

The Phoenix of Silicon Valley: Steve Jobs and the Power of Failure

One of the most iconic examples of transforming failure into opportunity is the story of Steve Jobs, the visionary co-founder of Apple. In 1985, Jobs was ousted from the very company he helped create. The blow was devastating, stripping him of his identity as a leader and innovator. For many, such a public fall from grace might have signaled the end of a career. But Jobs saw it differently.

In the years following his departure, Jobs founded NeXT, a computer company aimed at revolutionizing education and business technology. Though NeXT itself did not achieve commercial success, it became the crucible in which Jobs honed his design philosophy and business acumen. During this period, he also acquired Pixar, a fledgling animation studio struggling to find its footing. Under Jobs's guidance, Pixar transformed into a creative powerhouse, producing the world's first computer-animated feature film, *Toy Story*.

When Jobs eventually returned to Apple in 1997, he brought with him the lessons learned from his failures. His experiences outside the company had deepened his vision, enabling him to lead Apple into a new era of groundbreaking innovation with products like the iMac, iPod, and iPhone. Reflecting on this period, Jobs famously said, "Getting fired from Apple was the best thing that could have ever happened to me. The heaviness of being successful was replaced by the lightness of being a beginner again."

Jobs's story underscores a profound truth: failure is not the end but the beginning of reinvention. By reframing setbacks as opportunities for growth and experimentation, we can emerge stronger, wiser, and better equipped for future challenges.

Adversity as Innovation's Catalyst: The Story of Spanx

Sometimes, the seeds of opportunity are sown in the most unlikely of circumstances. For Sara Blakely, the founder of Spanx, adversity came in the form of rejection and frustration. Blakely had spent years working as a salesperson, enduring countless "no's" while pitching fax machines door-to-door. But it was a personal frustration—her inability to find comfortable and flattering undergarments—that sparked her entrepreneurial journey.

Blakely's lack of formal business training or fashion design experience might have seemed like insurmountable obstacles. Instead, she reframed these challenges as advantages, allowing her to think creatively and approach the problem from a fresh perspective. With a pair of scissors and a vision, she invented the prototype for Spanx, a product that would revolutionize women's shapewear.

What sets Blakely's story apart is her resilience in the face of rejection. When male investors failed to grasp the need for her product, she persisted, ultimately securing a manufacturer and launching Spanx with her own savings. Today, Spanx is a global brand, and Blakely is celebrated as one of the world's most successful self-made entrepreneurs. Her journey illustrates how adversity, when approached with determination and creativity, can lead to transformative breakthroughs.

The Alchemy of Perspective: Turning Setbacks into Growth

Both Jobs and Blakely share a common trait: the ability to see potential where others see failure. This mindset is rooted in the belief that challenges are not barriers but gateways to innovation. Adopting such a perspective requires us to shift our focus from what is lost to what can be gained.

Consider the Great Depression of the 1930s, a period of profound economic hardship that forced individuals and businesses to rethink their strategies for survival. While many faltered under the weight of uncertainty, some thrived by identifying emerging needs and pivoting their approaches. One such example is Procter & Gamble, which embraced the rising popularity of radio to create soap operas—a marketing innovation that solidified its brand presence and connected it with millions of households.

The lesson here is clear: adversity often reveals opportunities that were previously hidden. By examining challenges through the lens of curiosity and possibility, we can uncover paths to growth and reinvention.

Practical Applications: Cultivating Opportunity-Seeking Skills

Reframing difficulty as opportunity is not reserved for entrepreneurs or historical figures—it is a skill that anyone can cultivate. The first step is to recognize that adversity is a natural part of life, not a personal failing. Rather than viewing challenges as punishments, approach them as puzzles waiting to be solved.

A practical exercise involves asking three transformative questions when faced with a setback:

1. *What can I learn from this situation?*

2. *How can this experience make me stronger or more capable?*

3. *What new possibilities does this challenge present?*

These questions shift the narrative from one of defeat to one of growth, allowing us to see beyond immediate discomfort to the potential for long-term benefits.

Another powerful practice is cultivating gratitude for adversity. While it may seem counterintuitive, finding gratitude in difficult moments can unlock a deeper sense of purpose and resilience. By focusing on the lessons gained rather than the losses endured, we develop a mindset that thrives on transformation.

Embracing the Opportunity Within

Challenges are inevitable, but how we choose to perceive them defines their impact. For those willing to look beyond the surface, difficulty becomes an opportunity—a chance to learn, innovate, and grow. Steve Jobs's reinvention, Sara Blakely's entrepreneurial vision, and the resilience of countless others remind us that even in the darkest moments, opportunity exists for those who dare to see it.

Adopting this perspective is not merely a strategy for success; it is a philosophy for life. By seeking the silver linings within our struggles, we turn adversity into the catalyst for our greatest achievements. The power to transform challenges into opportunities lies not in external circumstances but within ourselves—a truth that empowers us to face life's trials with courage, creativity, and optimism.

Historical Perspectives on Adversity

Throughout history, adversity has been the crucible in which the mettle of leaders and movements has been tested and forged. It is not merely the existence of challenges but the ability to navigate them with courage, vision, and adaptability that distinguishes great leadership. By examining the lives and decisions of historical figures like Winston Churchill and Mahatma Gandhi, we gain valuable insights into how perspective shapes not only individual destinies but the fate of nations.

Winston Churchill: The Steadfastness of Vision in the Face of Darkness

Few moments in modern history were as fraught with peril as Britain's stand against Nazi Germany during World War II. As bombs fell over London and the possibility of invasion loomed, Winston Churchill emerged as a beacon of resolve. His speeches—punctuated by his unwavering declaration that Britain would "never surrender"—inspired a nation to endure its darkest hour.

Churchill's resilience was rooted in his ability to frame adversity as an opportunity for greatness. He did not minimize the severity of the threat; instead, he contextualized it within the broader narrative of human history. "To each, there comes in their lifetime a special moment," Churchill said, "when they are figuratively tapped on the shoulder and offered the chance to do a very special thing." For him, the war was Britain's moment to prove its mettle.

Churchill's perspective enabled him to galvanize not only his people but also international allies. He reframed the struggle not simply as a fight for British survival but as a battle for the preservation of freedom and civilization itself. His speeches, laced with humor, resolve, and unshakable confidence, infused the British public with a sense of purpose even amid nightly air raids and staggering losses.

The lesson from Churchill's leadership is clear: when faced with adversity, leaders must define the narrative. By framing challenges as opportunities for unity, growth, or moral triumph, they can inspire action and resilience even in the most trying times.

Mahatma Gandhi: Transforming Resistance into a Force for Liberation

Halfway across the world, another leader faced adversity of a different kind: colonial oppression. Mahatma Gandhi's leadership during India's struggle for independence against British rule exemplifies how reframing challenges can transform a movement.

Gandhi understood that the British Empire derived much of its power from violence and control. Instead of meeting force with force, he reframed resistance as a moral and spiritual act. His philosophy of *satyagraha*, or truth-force, positioned nonviolent resistance as the most powerful weapon against tyranny. For Gandhi, adversity was not a burden to be endured passively but an opportunity to demonstrate the strength of conviction and moral superiority.

The Salt March of 1930 is a vivid example of Gandhi's approach. At first glance, the British monopoly on salt seemed an insurmountable symbol of colonial exploitation. However, Gandhi reframed it as a rallying point for resistance. By marching 240 miles to the sea to make salt in defiance of British law, Gandhi galvanized millions of Indians, drawing international attention to their plight.

This act of reframing was not limited to physical resistance. Gandhi also encouraged his followers to embrace adversity as a teacher, urging them to find strength and unity in their shared struggle. He wrote, "Strength does not come from physical capacity. It comes from an indomitable will." His perspective transformed suffering into a collective source of empowerment, making it the foundation for one of history's most significant liberation movements.

Shared Themes: Framing Adversity as Purpose

Despite the stark differences in their challenges, Churchill and Gandhi shared a profound understanding of how perspective could transform adversity. For both leaders, reframing struggle as an opportunity to embody higher values—freedom, resilience, and truth—turned daunting challenges into sources of collective strength.

Churchill's framing of the war as a moral imperative rallied a nation, while Gandhi's vision of adversity as a spiritual calling united a people. In both cases, their perspectives empowered those they led to find meaning in hardship, enabling them to persevere against overwhelming odds.

Lessons for Modern Challenges

What do the experiences of Churchill and Gandhi teach us about facing adversity today? First, they remind us that perspective is not passive; it is an active choice. By framing challenges within a broader narrative of purpose or growth, we can transcend the immediate pain of adversity to focus on what truly matters.

Second, they highlight the importance of clarity and vision. Both leaders offered their people a sense of direction and meaning, transforming individual struggles into a shared mission. This principle is as relevant to modern workplaces and communities as it is to historical movements. When leaders articulate a clear purpose and inspire others to see challenges as opportunities, they foster resilience and collective strength.

Finally, their stories underscore the transformative power of aligning adversity with higher values. Whether it is a global crisis or a personal setback, framing the struggle as a chance to embody courage, perseverance, or innovation can turn even the most daunting challenges into opportunities for growth.

The Perspective That Endures

History's greatest leaders have shown us that adversity is not the enemy; it is the proving ground of vision and character. Winston Churchill's resolute defiance and Mahatma Gandhi's peaceful resistance remind us that the way we frame challenges determines their impact on our lives. By viewing adversity not as an insurmountable obstacle but as a crucible for growth, we can rise above the hardships that threaten to define us.

Perspective, then, is more than a tool for survival—it is the lens through which we shape our destinies. When we choose to see opportunity within difficulty, we align ourselves with a timeless truth: that the power to endure and thrive lies not in the absence of adversity but in our response to it.

Practical Steps to Reframe Challenges

The ability to reframe challenges is not a rare talent possessed by a fortunate few—it is a skill that can be learned, practiced, and mastered. By adopting practical strategies to shift perspective, we can transform moments of hardship into opportunities for growth, resilience, and reinvention. These techniques are grounded in both historical wisdom and modern psychology, offering a roadmap for navigating the inevitable struggles of life with clarity and strength.

Step 1: Pause and Reassess the Situation

When adversity strikes, our immediate reaction is often shaped by emotion. Fear, frustration, or anger can cloud judgment, making challenges appear more overwhelming than they truly are. The first step to reframing any challenge is to pause, creating space to reassess the situation with a clear mind.

Consider Abraham Lincoln during the early years of the American Civil War. Faced with mounting defeats and criticism, Lincoln was known for his measured approach to decision-making. He often sought solitude to reflect, write, and analyze the broader implications of each challenge. This deliberate pause allowed him to reframe setbacks not as signs of failure but as opportunities to recalibrate strategies and renew resolve.

Modern neuroscience supports the value of this practice. Pausing activates the brain's prefrontal cortex, the area responsible for rational thinking and problem-solving, allowing us to shift from reactive emotions to intentional responses. To cultivate this habit, consider incorporating mindfulness techniques such as deep breathing or journaling. These practices create a buffer between the challenge and your reaction, enabling you to approach the situation with greater clarity.

Step 2: Reframe Through Gratitude

Gratitude may seem like an unlikely tool for reframing adversity, but its transformative power lies in its ability to shift focus from what is lost to what remains. When we choose to acknowledge the positives within a challenging situation, we create space for hope and resilience.

During his imprisonment on Robben Island, Nelson Mandela endured years of isolation and hardship. Yet, he chose to focus on the lessons he could extract from his circumstances. Mandela expressed gratitude for the opportunity to deepen his understanding of his adversaries and strengthen his resolve to lead with compassion. This reframing not only sustained him through decades of struggle but also shaped the foundation for post-apartheid reconciliation.

For modern readers, practicing gratitude can be as simple as listing three things you appreciate each day, even in the midst of difficulty. By training your mind to seek positives, you reinforce a perspective that sees challenges as temporary and growth as inevitable.

Step 3: Redefine the Narrative

The stories we tell ourselves about adversity have a profound impact on how we experience it. A challenge framed as insurmountable becomes a self-fulfilling prophecy, while a challenge reframed as a stepping stone opens the door to possibility. Rewriting the narrative of adversity involves asking empowering questions: *What can I learn from this? How can this make me stronger?*

Consider Thomas Edison's perspective on failure. When asked about the thousands of unsuccessful attempts to create the lightbulb, Edison famously responded, "I have not failed. I've just found 10,000 ways that won't work." By reframing failure as progress, Edison turned what could have been a source of discouragement into a driver of relentless innovation.

To apply this in your own life, consciously identify and challenge negative narratives. Replace them with stories that emphasize growth, resilience, and the potential for future success. For example, instead of saying, "I failed at this project," reframe it as, "This project taught me valuable lessons I can apply moving forward."

Step 4: Focus on What You Can Control

One of the most paralyzing aspects of adversity is the feeling of helplessness. However, as Marcus Aurelius reminds us, "You have power over your mind—not outside events. Realize this, and you will find strength." The key to overcoming this paralysis lies in focusing on what is within your control, no matter how small it may seem.

During the Allied evacuation at Dunkirk in 1940, British military leaders faced overwhelming odds. Instead of succumbing to despair over what was uncontrollable—the enemy's advance—they focused on what they could control: organizing one of the most remarkable evacuations in history. This shift in focus not only saved thousands of lives but also galvanized British morale, reframing the event as a testament to resilience rather than defeat.

To adopt this principle in your own life, break challenges into manageable steps. Identify what actions are within your control and channel your energy toward them. By doing so, you regain a sense of agency and forward momentum, even in the face of uncertainty.

Step 5: Seek Meaning in the Struggle

The ultimate reframing of adversity is finding meaning within it. Viktor Frankl's experience in concentration camps, as detailed in *Man's Search for Meaning*, illustrates this principle with profound clarity. Frankl observed that those who found purpose in their suffering—whether it was the hope of reuniting with loved ones or contributing to a greater cause—were more likely to endure.

Finding meaning does not erase the pain of adversity, but it transforms it into something bearable, even transformative. For Frankl, the search for meaning was not a luxury but a survival strategy. His approach teaches us that even the most difficult experiences can contribute to our growth, wisdom, and empathy.

In practical terms, finding meaning may involve connecting your struggle to a larger goal or value. Ask yourself, *How can this experience help me grow? How might it enable me to contribute to others?* These questions shift focus from the hardship itself to the opportunities it creates for personal and collective transformation.

Step 6: Surround Yourself with Perspective-Enhancing Voices

Lastly, the people we surround ourselves with play a significant role in shaping our perspective. During moments of adversity, seeking out mentors, role models, or supportive communities can provide fresh insights and encouragement.

When Theodore Roosevelt faced personal tragedies and political setbacks early in his career, he found solace and renewal in the company of trusted friends and advisors. Their perspectives helped him navigate loss and reframe his challenges, ultimately paving the way for his rise to the presidency.

For contemporary readers, this might mean

joining support groups, engaging with inspiring literature, or seeking mentorship. By immersing yourself in environments that encourage resilience and growth, you reinforce the mindset needed to reframe challenges constructively.

Transforming Adversity into Opportunity

Reframing challenges is not about denying the reality of hardship—it is about transforming the way we engage with it. By pausing to reassess, practicing gratitude, redefining narratives, focusing on controllable actions, seeking meaning, and surrounding ourselves with supportive voices, we cultivate a perspective that empowers rather than paralyzes.

The power to reframe challenges lies within all of us. It requires intention, practice, and a willingness to see beyond immediate discomfort to the possibilities that adversity holds. By applying these practical steps, we not only navigate difficulties with greater resilience but also discover within them the seeds of growth, strength, and reinvention.

CHAPTER 2: THE ART OF LETTING GO – RELEASING WHAT NO LONGER SERVES

Understanding the Need to Let Go

Growth, whether personal or societal, often requires a willingness to release what no longer serves us. Yet letting go is rarely easy. Familiar patterns, even when outdated or detrimental, offer a sense of stability. It takes courage to confront the discomfort of change and the uncertainty of what lies ahead. However, history and human experience reveal that holding onto the past can stifle progress, while letting go opens the door to transformation.

The Weight of Tradition: Lessons from the Fall of Feudalism

For centuries, feudalism dominated medieval Europe, shaping social, economic, and political structures. Lords owned the land, peasants worked it, and society functioned within rigid hierarchies. While this system provided order during a time of widespread instability, it became increasingly unsustainable as economies evolved and populations grew.

By the late Middle Ages, cracks began to appear in the feudal structure. The Black Death decimated the population, creating labor shortages that undermined the power of the landowning elite. Simultaneously, the rise of trade and urbanization introduced new opportunities for wealth and mobility. Despite these changes, many clung to the feudal system, resisting shifts that threatened their traditional way of life.

The decline of feudalism was not a sudden collapse but a slow unraveling, marked by conflicts and upheavals. Revolts like the English Peasants' Revolt of 1381 demonstrated the growing dissatisfaction with feudal obligations. Over time, monarchs and emerging nation-states began to consolidate power, replacing feudal loyalty with centralized governance. The transition was painful and chaotic, but it paved the way for democratic principles, modern economies, and individual freedoms that would define the centuries to come.

The lesson from feudalism's decline is clear: holding onto outdated systems can hinder progress, while letting go—though uncomfortable—creates space for innovation and growth. This principle applies not only to societies but also to individuals. Just as feudalism eventually gave way to more equitable and dynamic systems, we must be willing to release habits, beliefs, and practices that no longer align with our evolving needs and aspirations.

The Burden of Outdated Beliefs

Beliefs are powerful. They shape our perceptions, guide our decisions, and influence how we engage with the world. Yet, not all beliefs stand the test of time. Some, rooted in fear or ignorance, can become barriers to progress. Letting go of these outdated beliefs requires introspection and a willingness to challenge long-held assumptions.

Consider the transition from geocentrism to heliocentrism in the 16th and 17th centuries. For centuries, the belief that Earth was the center of the universe dominated scientific thought, supported by religious doctrine and cultural tradition. This worldview provided a sense of order and significance, reinforcing humanity's perceived centrality in the cosmos.

When Copernicus, and later Galileo, proposed that the Earth revolved around the sun, their ideas were met with fierce resistance. To accept heliocentrism meant relinquishing not only a scientific theory but also a worldview deeply intertwined with identity and meaning. Despite the controversy, the eventual acceptance of heliocentrism marked a turning point in human understanding, ushering in the Scientific Revolution and challenging humanity to embrace a broader, more complex view of the universe.

This shift highlights the importance of questioning beliefs that no longer align with evidence or progress. Just as societies benefited from letting go of geocentric models, individuals can grow by examining and releasing limiting beliefs. Whether it's a fear of failure, a rigid definition of success, or an inherited bias, shedding these outdated perspectives allows us to move forward with clarity and purpose.

The Courage to Release

Letting go is inherently a courageous act. It requires us to confront the discomfort of uncertainty and the fear of loss. Yet, history demonstrates that the act of releasing is often the precursor to profound transformation.

The American Revolution offers a compelling example of this principle. For decades, the American colonies operated under British rule, bound by economic regulations and political oversight. While the relationship offered stability and protection, it also imposed restrictions that stifled autonomy and growth.

When tensions reached a breaking point, the colonies faced a critical decision: continue under British rule or risk everything in the pursuit of independence. Choosing the latter meant letting go of the security and familiarity of colonial governance—a daunting prospect fraught with uncertainty. Yet, this act of release was the catalyst for the birth of a new nation, founded on principles of self-governance and individual liberty.

The American Revolution reminds us that letting go often involves short-term discomfort for long-term gain. Whether on a societal or personal level, releasing what no longer serves us is a necessary step toward realizing our potential.

The Price of Holding On

While the benefits of letting go are clear, the cost of holding on can be equally profound. Clinging to outdated systems, beliefs, or habits can lead to stagnation, frustration, and missed opportunities. The collapse of ancient empires, the decline of industries resistant to innovation, and personal stories of burnout all underscore the dangers of resisting change.

Take the story of Kodak, the iconic photography company. In the late 20th century, Kodak dominated the film industry, but it failed to adapt to the rise of digital photography—a technology it had ironically helped pioneer. Instead of embracing the shift, Kodak clung to its traditional business model, believing that film would remain the dominant medium. This reluctance to let go led to the company's decline, serving as a cautionary tale for businesses and individuals alike.

The Kodak story illustrates a universal truth: when we resist the need to release what no longer serves us, we risk being left behind. Growth requires adaptability, and adaptability begins with the willingness to let go.

A Path Forward

Letting go is not about abandoning the past but about making room for the future. It is a process of discerning what to keep and what to release, guided by a commitment to growth and alignment with one's values. By understanding the need to let go, we empower ourselves to move forward with purpose, clarity, and resilience.

As we continue through this chapter, we will explore how letting go has shaped some of history's greatest transitions and how it can serve as a powerful tool for personal reinvention. The art of releasing is not an act of weakness but a profound expression of strength, rooted in the belief that the best is yet to come.

Lessons from Great Transitions

The story of human progress is one of constant reinvention, marked by pivotal transitions that redefined societies and transformed civilizations. At the heart of these great shifts lies a willingness—or sometimes an unwillingness—to let go of old paradigms. History shows that letting go of outdated systems and beliefs is not just a choice but a necessity for growth. Two profound examples of such transitions are the Renaissance and the shift from superstition to science. Both illustrate how releasing the grip of the past can illuminate the path to a brighter, more enlightened future.

The Renaissance: Reclaiming and Reimagining Knowledge

The Renaissance, spanning roughly the 14th to the 17th centuries, stands as one of the most remarkable transitions in human history. Emerging from the shadows of the Middle Ages, this era marked a profound cultural and intellectual awakening that reshaped art, science, and philosophy. At its core, the Renaissance was a movement of rediscovery and release—reclaiming the wisdom of antiquity while breaking free from the constraints of medieval thought.

For centuries, much of Europe's intellectual life had been dominated by scholasticism, a system that sought to reconcile classical philosophy with religious dogma. While scholasticism had its merits, it often stifled creativity and inquiry, binding knowledge to rigid frameworks. The Renaissance challenged this approach, fueled by a renewed interest in the classical works of ancient Greece and Rome. Thinkers like Petrarch and Erasmus advocated for a return to the *ad fontes*—the original sources—urging scholars to engage directly with ancient texts rather than relying on filtered interpretations.

This intellectual liberation was not without resistance. The medieval worldview, deeply rooted in religious tradition, clashed with the Renaissance's emphasis on humanism and secular inquiry. Yet, the willingness to release outdated constraints led to extraordinary advancements. Artists like Michelangelo and Leonardo da Vinci redefined the possibilities of creative expression, blending scientific precision with aesthetic brilliance. Scientists like Copernicus and Galileo challenged long-held beliefs about the cosmos, setting the stage for the Scientific Revolution.

The Renaissance teaches us that progress often requires both the courage to let go of limiting frameworks and the vision to imagine new possibilities. By releasing the intellectual strictures of the past, this era illuminated the vast potential of human creativity and reason, reminding us that true growth arises from the interplay of preservation and reinvention.

The Scientific Revolution: Breaking Free from Superstition

The shift from superstition to science is another profound example of the power of letting go. For much of human history, explanations of natural phenomena were steeped in superstition, myth, and religious interpretation. Thunderstorms were attributed to the wrath of gods, plagues to divine punishment, and celestial movements to mysterious forces. While these beliefs provided comfort and order in an unpredictable world, they also hindered the pursuit of empirical understanding.

The Scientific Revolution of the 16th and 17th centuries marked a radical departure from this worldview. Pioneers like Francis Bacon, René Descartes, and Isaac Newton championed a new approach to knowledge—one grounded in observation, experimentation, and critical inquiry. This transition required a collective willingness to question long-held assumptions and embrace uncertainty.

Galileo's struggle exemplifies the tension of this era. His advocacy for heliocentrism, the idea that the Earth orbits the sun, challenged centuries of geocentric belief upheld by religious authorities. Galileo's findings, based on meticulous observation and mathematical reasoning, represented a seismic shift in human understanding of the universe. Yet, his ideas were met with vehement opposition, culminating in his trial and condemnation by the Inquisition.

Despite such resistance, the Scientific Revolution ultimately triumphed, laying the foundation for modern science and technology. By letting go of superstition, humanity unlocked a deeper understanding of the natural world, paving the way for advancements in medicine, engineering, and countless other fields. This transition highlights the power of curiosity and skepticism as tools for progress. It reminds us that growth often requires challenging the familiar and venturing into the unknown.

The Cost of Clinging to the Past

While the Renaissance and the Scientific Revolution demonstrate the transformative power of letting go, history also warns of the consequences of resistance to change. The decline of once-mighty empires, the stagnation of institutions, and the collapse of outdated industries all underscore the dangers of clinging to the past.

Consider the Ottoman Empire in its later centuries. Once a beacon of cultural and scientific innovation, the empire struggled to adapt to the changing dynamics of global politics and technology. Efforts to preserve traditional systems of governance and military organization, while noble in intent, left the empire vulnerable to external pressures and internal decay. The reluctance to let go of antiquated structures ultimately contributed to its downfall, serving as a cautionary tale for societies and individuals alike.

Lessons for Personal and Collective Growth

The transitions of the Renaissance and the Scientific Revolution offer timeless lessons that extend beyond historical analysis. On a personal level, they remind us that growth often requires shedding the familiar to embrace the unknown. Just as Renaissance thinkers released the constraints of medieval thought to explore the depths of human potential, we too must examine the beliefs and habits that shape our lives, asking whether they serve our highest aspirations.

Collectively, these transitions highlight the importance of openness and adaptability in navigating change. As societies face challenges such as climate change, technological disruption, and social inequality, the ability to let go of outdated systems and embrace innovative solutions will determine the course of the future. The courage to release is not just a historical necessity—it is a contemporary imperative.

Embracing the Spirit of Transition

The great transitions of history remind us that letting go is not an act of destruction but of creation. By releasing the constraints of the past, we make room for new ideas, perspectives, and possibilities. The Renaissance and the Scientific Revolution stand as testaments to the transformative power of this process, challenging us to approach change not with fear but with curiosity and hope.

As we navigate the complexities of modern life, these lessons remain as relevant as ever. Whether we are seeking personal growth, driving societal progress, or confronting global challenges, the art of letting go offers a path to reinvention and renewal. In the words of Galileo, "You cannot teach a man anything; you can only help him find it within himself." By releasing what no longer serves us, we uncover the boundless potential that lies within.

Personal Reinvention Through Release

Reinvention is one of the most profound acts of letting go, requiring individuals to release not just habits or beliefs but sometimes entire identities. It is a process marked by courage, vulnerability, and an unwavering commitment to growth. Those who successfully reinvent themselves remind us that change is not only possible but transformative. By shedding what no longer serves them, they uncover deeper purpose, creativity, and fulfillment.

The Courage to Walk Away: Howard Schultz and the Starbucks Story

When Howard Schultz first encountered Starbucks in the early 1980s, it was a modest coffee retailer in Seattle with a handful of locations. Schultz, working as the vice president of a housewares company, was captivated by the company's passion for high-quality coffee. Yet, when he proposed expanding Starbucks into a café-style experience inspired by Italian espresso bars, the founders rejected his vision.

Faced with this setback, Schultz made a pivotal decision: he chose to leave the security of his corporate role to pursue his dream independently. Launching his own coffee business, Il Giornale, Schultz brought his vision to life, blending premium coffee with an inviting atmosphere. Eventually, he acquired Starbucks and transformed it into the global powerhouse it is today.

Schultz's story illustrates the power of letting go—releasing the comfort of an established career to chase an untested idea. It also underscores the importance of aligning one's actions with a deeper sense of purpose. By letting go of the familiar, Schultz not only redefined his own path but also revolutionized the way the world experiences coffee.

Embracing the Unknown: Oprah Winfrey's Journey to Reinvention

For many, Oprah Winfrey's name is synonymous with success. Yet, her path to becoming a media icon was far from linear. Early in her career, Oprah faced challenges that might have discouraged a less determined individual. After a brief stint as a television news anchor, she was fired, with her employer citing her emotional delivery as a poor fit for the role.

Instead of viewing this setback as a failure, Oprah reframed it as an opportunity to pivot. Recognizing that her strengths lay in connecting with audiences on a personal level, she transitioned into daytime talk shows. This shift allowed her to embrace her authentic self, creating a space where empathy and vulnerability became assets rather than liabilities.

The success of *The Oprah Winfrey Show* was not just a testament to Oprah's talent but to her willingness to let go of traditional expectations and redefine her career. Her story reminds us that reinvention often involves leaning into our unique qualities, even when they deviate from conventional norms. By releasing societal expectations and embracing authenticity, Oprah built a legacy that transcends media, inspiring millions to pursue their own paths.

Shedding Old Identities: Entrepreneurs Who Found Freedom

The world of entrepreneurship is rich with stories of reinvention, many of which begin with the difficult decision to leave behind established careers. For Sara Blakely, the founder of Spanx, the journey began in the aisles of office supply stores, where she sold fax machines door-to-door. While her job provided financial stability, it left her unfulfilled.

Blakely's decision to pursue entrepreneurship was fueled by a simple idea: creating a better undergarment for women. With no formal background in fashion or business, she took a leap of faith, investing her savings to develop a prototype. Today, Spanx is a global brand, and Blakely is celebrated as one of the world's most successful self-made entrepreneurs.

Her story illustrates the importance of releasing old identities to embrace new possibilities. Letting go of the security of a corporate career allowed Blakely to explore her creativity, take risks, and ultimately achieve a level of success she never imagined. Her journey underscores a universal truth: reinvention requires trust in oneself and the courage to venture into the unknown.

The Philosophy of Reinvention

At its core, personal reinvention is an act of liberation. It involves recognizing that the roles we play—employee, leader, caretaker—are not fixed but fluid. As we grow, our goals, values, and passions evolve, often prompting us to re-evaluate the identities we have built. While this process can be uncomfortable, it also offers a profound opportunity to align with our true selves.

Philosophers like Søren Kierkegaard have long emphasized the importance of self-reinvention. Kierkegaard argued that authenticity requires us to continuously examine and redefine our choices, shedding what no longer aligns with our deeper sense of purpose. This process, though challenging, is essential for living a fulfilling and meaningful life.

In modern psychology, the concept of a "growth mindset" reinforces this philosophy. Coined by Dr. Carol Dweck, a growth mindset is the belief that our abilities and identities are not fixed but capable of expansion through effort and learning. By adopting this perspective, we open ourselves to the possibility of reinvention, embracing change as an opportunity rather than a threat.

Practical Insights for Personal Reinvention

While the stories of Schultz, Winfrey, and Blakely may seem extraordinary, the principles of reinvention are accessible to everyone. The first step is self-awareness—identifying the aspects of your life that no longer serve you and the aspirations that inspire you. Reflecting on questions like *What am I holding onto out of fear?* and *What would I pursue if I weren't afraid to fail?* can provide clarity and direction.

Next comes the willingness to release. Letting go of old identities, habits, or beliefs is rarely easy. It often involves facing uncertainty, challenging societal expectations, and embracing vulnerability. Yet, as history and experience demonstrate, the act of release is a prerequisite for transformation.

Finally, reinvention requires action. Whether it's pursuing a new career, adopting a healthier lifestyle, or embracing a creative passion, taking concrete steps toward your goals is essential. Progress may be slow, and setbacks are inevitable, but each step reinforces your commitment to growth and authenticity.

The Gift of Starting Anew

Reinvention is not a rejection of the past but a celebration of the possibility that lies ahead. By letting go of what no longer serves us, we create space for new experiences, relationships, and opportunities that align with our evolving selves.

The stories of Schultz, Winfrey, and Blakely remind us that reinvention is not reserved for the extraordinary—it is a path available to all who are willing to embrace it. Whether you are seeking to transform your career, relationships, or sense of self, the act of letting go holds the key to unlocking your potential. In the words of poet Mary Oliver, "Tell me, what is it you plan to do with your one wild and precious life?" The answer begins with the courage to release and the willingness to begin again.

Tools for Letting Go

Letting go is often portrayed as a simple act of release, but in reality, it is a deeply personal and deliberate process. It requires clarity, courage, and practical strategies to identify what no longer serves us and to move forward with purpose. Whether it involves decluttering physical spaces, releasing emotional baggage, or breaking free from outdated mental frameworks, the art of letting go empowers us to live more authentically and intentionally. In this section, we explore tools and techniques that help navigate this journey, blending historical insights with actionable guidance.

The Power of Self-Reflection

The first step in letting go is understanding what needs to be released. This requires self-reflection, an honest examination of the habits, beliefs, and attachments that shape our lives. Self-reflection acts as a mirror, revealing the areas where we may be holding on out of fear, comfort, or societal expectations.

Consider the story of Siddhartha Gautama, who would become known as the Buddha. Born into luxury as a prince, Siddhartha lived a life shielded from suffering. Yet, upon encountering the realities of aging, illness, and death, he recognized the emptiness of his material comforts. In a profound act of letting go, he renounced his royal status and embarked on a spiritual quest, seeking enlightenment and liberation from suffering.

Siddhartha's journey underscores the importance of questioning what truly serves us. Modern readers can engage in this process through journaling, meditation, or introspective questions like:

- *What am I holding onto that feels heavy or draining?*

- *Does this belief, habit, or possession align with my current values and goals?*

- *What would my life look like if I released this attachment?*

By cultivating self-awareness, we gain clarity on what to release and why, laying the foundation for meaningful change.

Decluttering Physical Spaces

Physical clutter often mirrors emotional and mental clutter. Letting go of possessions that no longer serve a purpose can be a transformative act, creating space not only in our environments but also in our minds.

The Japanese philosophy of *ma*, which emphasizes the value of empty space, provides a compelling perspective on decluttering. In Japanese culture, empty spaces are not seen as voids but as opportunities for creativity and potential. This principle is embodied in Marie Kondo's *KonMari Method*, which encourages individuals to keep only the items that "spark joy." By releasing possessions that no longer bring value, individuals create environments that reflect their authentic selves.

This practice is not about minimalism for its own sake but about aligning our external surroundings with our internal priorities. As we let go of unnecessary possessions, we often experience a sense of liberation, gaining clarity and focus for what truly matters.

Releasing Emotional Baggage

Emotional attachments—whether to past experiences, relationships, or self-perceptions—can weigh us down, preventing us from moving forward. Letting go of emotional baggage involves both forgiveness and acceptance, two processes that are as liberating as they are challenging.

One powerful example comes from Nelson Mandela, who endured 27 years of imprisonment under South Africa's apartheid regime.

Upon his release, Mandela chose to forgive his captors, recognizing that holding onto anger and resentment would only perpetuate his suffering. He famously said, "Resentment is like drinking poison and then hoping it will kill your enemies." By releasing emotional pain, Mandela freed himself to focus on reconciliation and rebuilding his nation.

For those seeking to release emotional baggage, practices such as therapy, mindfulness, or writing letters (even if they are never sent) can provide catharsis and clarity. The goal is not to erase the past but to integrate it, allowing it to inform but not define our present and future.

Letting Go of Mental Frameworks

Our minds are powerful, but they can also trap us in limiting beliefs and unproductive thought patterns. Letting go of outdated mental frameworks requires conscious effort to challenge and replace these patterns with more empowering perspectives.

Cognitive behavioral therapy (CBT), a widely practiced psychological approach, offers valuable tools for this process. At its core, CBT involves identifying negative thought patterns, questioning their validity, and replacing them with constructive alternatives. For example, a belief like, "I'll never succeed because I've failed before," can be reexamined through a lens of growth: "Failure is a stepping stone to success, and I can learn from past experiences."

Historical figures like Eleanor Roosevelt exemplify the power of reframing mental narratives. Born into a family that doubted her abilities, Eleanor struggled with self-esteem for much of her early life. However, by actively challenging these internalized doubts and embracing her unique voice, she became one of the most influential first ladies in American history, championing human rights and social reform.

To let go of limiting mental frameworks, begin by cultivating self-compassion. Recognize that growth is a journey, and perfection is neither attainable nor necessary. By practicing kindness toward yourself and embracing a mindset of curiosity, you create the mental flexibility needed to release old patterns and adopt new ones.

Building Rituals of Release

Letting go can be deeply symbolic, and rituals provide a powerful way to mark this process. Whether it's burning old journals, donating possessions, or engaging in a ceremonial act of release, rituals create a sense of closure and intention.

One contemporary example is the practice of writing down fears, regrets, or negative experiences on paper and then physically destroying it—by shredding, burning, or tearing it apart. This act serves as a tangible representation of releasing what no longer serves us, reinforcing our commitment to move forward.

Similarly, cultural traditions such as the Tibetan practice of *sand mandalas* embody the beauty of impermanence. Monks spend days creating intricate mandalas from colored sand, only to dismantle them upon completion, symbolizing the transient nature of life. These rituals remind us that release is not a loss but a natural and necessary part of life's cycles.

The Freedom to Move Forward

Letting go is an act of self-liberation. It is not about rejecting the past but about creating space for what comes next. By reflecting on what no longer serves us, decluttering our environments, releasing emotional burdens, challenging mental frameworks, and embracing symbolic rituals, we empower ourselves to live more fully and authentically.

The tools for letting go are as diverse as the individuals who use them. Whether you start with a single act of decluttering or embark on a profound journey of emotional release, each step is a testament to your commitment to growth. In the words of poet Anaïs Nin, "Life shrinks or expands in proportion to one's courage." Letting go is an act of courage, and in that courage lies the promise of expansion, transformation, and freedom.

CHAPTER 3: REINVENTION THROUGH ACTION – BUILDING MOMENTUM AMID CHANGE

The Importance of Action

Action is the heartbeat of reinvention. It transforms thought into reality, potential into progress, and hope into tangible results. In times of uncertainty, when the path forward seems unclear, action becomes even more critical. It is the mechanism through which we regain agency, overcome inertia, and create momentum. Throughout history, the individuals and teams who embraced action, even amid doubt and adversity, catalyzed extraordinary transformations. Their stories remind us that progress does not wait for perfect conditions—it begins with a single step.

The Wright Brothers: Taking Flight Through Action

The story of Orville and Wilbur Wright exemplifies the transformative power of action. At the turn of the 20th century, the idea of human flight was seen as a fantastical dream, pursued by a handful of enthusiasts. The Wright brothers, bicycle makers from Dayton, Ohio, were hardly the most likely candidates to achieve this milestone. They lacked formal engineering education, financial backing, and access to advanced technology. Yet, what they possessed in abundance was an unwavering commitment to action.

The Wright brothers approached the challenge of flight methodically, conducting countless experiments and refining their designs through trial and error. They built wind tunnels to test aerodynamics, designed their own engines, and meticulously documented every step of their process. Each failed attempt became a stepping stone, providing valuable data that brought them closer to success.

In 1903, at Kitty Hawk, North Carolina, the Wright brothers achieved what many deemed impossible: the first powered, controlled, and sustained flight of a heavier-than-air machine. This groundbreaking moment was not the result of luck or ideal conditions but the culmination of years of relentless action. Their story teaches us that even the most audacious goals can be realized when we commit to consistent, purposeful effort.

Thomas Edison: A Legacy of Persistence

Few individuals embody the importance of action as vividly as Thomas Edison. Over the course of his life, Edison amassed over 1,000 patents, a testament to his belief in the power of persistence and experimentation. Yet, his journey was far from smooth. One of his most iconic inventions, the electric lightbulb, required thousands of failed attempts before he discovered a viable filament material.

When asked about his repeated failures, Edison famously replied, "I have not failed. I've just found 10,000 ways that won't work." This perspective underscores a critical truth: action is not always about immediate success. Often, it is about learning, adapting, and iterating. Each attempt, regardless of its outcome, moves us closer to our goals.

Edison's success was rooted in his willingness to act in the face of uncertainty. He recognized that waiting for perfect conditions or flawless ideas would lead to stagnation. Instead, he embraced the process of discovery, understanding that progress is built on a foundation of action and experimentation.

The Philosophy of Action in Uncertain Times

In uncertain times, the instinct to wait for clarity or control can be paralyzing. However, history shows that action itself often creates clarity. By taking the first step, we gain new insights, build confidence, and uncover opportunities that were previously invisible.

Philosophers and thinkers have long emphasized the importance of action as a means of navigating uncertainty. Søren Kierkegaard, the father of existentialism, argued that action is essential to living authentically. "Life can only be understood backwards," he wrote, "but it must be lived forwards." This sentiment captures the paradox of uncertainty: while we may not fully comprehend the outcomes of our actions, it is through acting that we create meaning and direction.

Similarly, modern psychology highlights the relationship between action and motivation. Contrary to the belief that we must feel motivated before taking action, research suggests the reverse is often true. Action generates momentum, which in turn fuels motivation. This concept, known as the "progress principle," reveals that even small steps can ignite a cycle of forward movement, making daunting challenges more manageable.

Practical Lessons from the Wright Brothers and Edison

The stories of the Wright brothers and Edison offer valuable lessons for those seeking to build momentum in their own lives. First, they remind us that action need not be grand or perfect. The Wright brothers began with simple kites and gliders, testing their theories in small, incremental ways. Edison's process was similarly iterative, with each prototype building on the lessons of the last.

Second, these stories emphasize the importance of resilience in the face of failure. Both the Wright brothers and Edison encountered setbacks that could have discouraged them from continuing. Instead, they reframed failure as an opportunity to learn and improve. This mindset allowed them to persevere, transforming obstacles into stepping stones.

Finally, their journeys highlight the value of curiosity and experimentation. By remaining open to new ideas and approaches, they were able to innovate and adapt, even when faced with uncertainty. This spirit of exploration is as relevant today as it was in their time, encouraging us to approach challenges with creativity and determination.

The Ripple Effect of Action

One of the most profound aspects of action is its ripple effect. When we take a step forward, we not only transform our own lives but also inspire and influence those around us. The Wright brothers' flight ignited a global aviation revolution, sparking advancements that would change the course of history. Edison's inventions laid the foundation for modern technology, shaping the way we live, work, and communicate.

On a smaller scale, individual acts of courage and initiative can create ripples within families, communities, and workplaces. By choosing to act, we set an example for others, demonstrating that progress is possible even in the face of uncertainty.

The Call to Act

Action is the bridge between aspiration and achievement. It is not the absence of doubt but the willingness to move forward despite it. In times of uncertainty, when the road ahead feels obscured, action provides a way to illuminate the path. Whether it's launching a new project, learning a new skill, or simply taking the first step toward a long-held dream, the act of doing creates momentum that carries us forward.

As the stories of the Wright brothers and Edison illustrate, progress is not reserved for the exceptional—it is accessible to anyone willing to act with purpose and persistence. By embracing the importance of action, we unlock our potential to reinvent ourselves and shape the future. In the words of Goethe, "Whatever you can do or dream you can, begin it. Boldness has genius, power, and magic in it." The time to act is now.

Overcoming Inertia

Inertia, the tendency to remain in a state of rest,

is as much a psychological challenge as it is a physical concept. The difficulty of starting something new often feels insurmountable, particularly when faced with uncertainty or fear. Yet, overcoming inertia is essential for reinvention, growth, and progress. To move forward, we must first address the barriers that hold us back, whether they stem from procrastination, fear of failure, or a lack of clarity. The good news is that inertia, while powerful, is not insurmountable. By understanding its roots, we can cultivate the tools to overcome it and step into action.

The Paralysis of Procrastination

Procrastination is perhaps the most common form of inertia. It is the act of delaying tasks despite knowing their importance, often driven by a combination of overwhelm, perfectionism, and fear. Left unchecked, procrastination creates a cycle of inaction, eroding confidence and amplifying stress.

Leonardo da Vinci's creative genius is often celebrated, but even he struggled with procrastination. Despite his remarkable accomplishments, da Vinci left many projects incomplete, including an ambitious plan to divert the Arno River. His patron, Ludovico Sforza, often lamented da Vinci's tendency to delay, distracted by new ideas or a desire for perfection.

Da Vinci's story illustrates an important point: even the most talented individuals are not immune to procrastination. However, his life also shows that overcoming inertia is possible when we focus on progress rather than perfection. Da Vinci's ability to complete masterpieces like the *Mona Lisa* and *The Last Supper* was rooted in his eventual willingness to begin, even when conditions were not ideal.

The lesson here is clear: action, no matter how small, is the antidote to procrastination. By breaking tasks into manageable steps and committing to the first step, we can disrupt the cycle of delay and build momentum.

The Shadow of Fear

Fear is another potent source of inertia, often disguised as logical caution or self-doubt. The fear of failure, criticism, or the unknown can paralyze even the most capable individuals, preventing them from taking risks or pursuing opportunities.

Consider the story of J.K. Rowling, who faced numerous rejections before achieving success with *Harry Potter and the Philosopher's Stone*. As a single mother living on welfare, Rowling could have easily succumbed to fear—fear of further rejection, fear of financial instability, or fear of inadequacy. Yet, she chose to act despite her doubts, sending her manuscript to multiple publishers until it found a home. Her courage to overcome inertia transformed her life and inspired millions around the world.

Rowling's journey highlights the importance of reframing fear. Rather than viewing it as a signal to stop, we can interpret fear as a sign of growth—an indicator that we are stepping out of our comfort zones. By acknowledging fear without letting it dictate our actions, we reclaim our agency and move forward with purpose.

The Illusion of Perfect Timing

One of the most pervasive myths contributing to inertia is the belief in perfect timing. Waiting for ideal conditions often becomes an excuse for in-action, as we convince ourselves that the "right moment" will eventually arrive. However, history reveals that most significant achievements were born not out of perfect circumstances but out of imperfect beginnings.

Take the example of Mahatma Gandhi, who led India's struggle for independence. Gandhi's decision to launch the Salt March in 1930—a peaceful protest against British salt laws—was met with skepticism. Critics argued that the timing was poor and the gesture symbolic rather than practical. Yet, Gandhi recognized that waiting for perfect conditions would lead to stagnation. His willingness to act in the face of uncertainty mobilized millions and marked a turning point in the independence movement.

Gandhi's leadership teaches us that progress often requires embracing imperfection. The conditions may never feel entirely right, but action creates momentum, which in turn generates opportunities and clarity.

Practical Steps to Break Free from Inertia

Overcoming inertia begins with self-awareness—recognizing the barriers that hold us back
and addressing them with intention. While each
individual's challenges are unique, certain strategies can help disrupt the cycle of inaction and
pave the way for forward movement.

One effective approach is the "two-minute rule,"
popularized by productivity expert David Allen.
The rule suggests that if a task takes less than
two minutes, it should be done immediately.
This principle not only eliminates small sources
of procrastination but also builds momentum
for tackling larger tasks.

Another strategy involves reframing large goals
into smaller, more manageable steps. Instead
of focusing on the daunting scope of a project,
identify the smallest actionable task and commit
to completing it. For instance, if writing a book
feels overwhelming, start by drafting a single
sentence or brainstorming ideas for a chapter.
Each small step reinforces the habit of action,
gradually dismantling inertia.

Lastly, accountability can be a powerful moti-
vator. Sharing your goals with a trusted friend,

mentor, or community creates a sense of responsibility and support, making it easier to stay committed to action.

The Role of Self-Compassion

While overcoming inertia requires effort, it is equally important to practice self-compassion. Many individuals become trapped in inertia not because of laziness but because of self-critical thoughts that erode confidence. Instead of berating ourselves for inaction, we can acknowledge our struggles with kindness and curiosity.

Research in psychology shows that self-compassion enhances resilience, motivation, and overall well-being. By treating ourselves with the same understanding we would offer a friend, we create a supportive inner dialogue that encourages action rather than paralyzing self-doubt.

From Inertia to Momentum

Breaking free from inertia is not about achieving instant transformation—it is about taking the first step. Whether it's sending an email, making a phone call, or setting aside five minutes to brainstorm, each action, no matter how small, disrupts the cycle of inaction and sets the stage for progress.

The stories of da Vinci, Rowling, and Gandhi remind us that inertia is a universal challenge, but it is not an insurmountable one. By addressing procrastination, reframing fear, and embracing imperfect beginnings, we unlock our potential to act with purpose and confidence.

Inertia may feel like an unyielding force, but its power diminishes with every step we take. Action, once begun, builds momentum, propelling us forward toward reinvention and growth. As the Chinese proverb wisely states, "The journey of a thousand miles begins with a single step." That step, however small, is the beginning of change.

Historical Models of Bold Action

Throughout history, moments of bold action have reshaped the world, transforming societies and redefining what is possible. These acts of courage often occurred in the face of uncertainty and resistance, yet their impact was profound.

The stories of those who dared to act—whether explorers during the Age of Discovery or industrial pioneers who revolutionized entire industries—serve as enduring reminders of the transformative power of bold action.

The Age of Discovery: Charting the Unknown

The Age of Discovery, spanning the 15th to the 17th centuries, was a period of unprecedented exploration. Driven by the promise of new trade routes, wealth, and knowledge, European explorers ventured into uncharted waters, often at great personal and national risk. Their journeys required not only physical courage but also bold action in the face of skepticism and fear of the unknown.

Christopher Columbus's first voyage to the Americas in 1492 exemplifies this spirit of bold action. Backed by the Spanish monarchy, Columbus set sail with the belief that he could reach Asia by crossing the Atlantic Ocean—a hypothesis met with doubt by many contemporaries. His journey was fraught with challenges, including uncertain navigation and the growing unrest of his crew. Yet, Columbus's willingness to act despite these uncertainties paved the way for the European exploration and colonization of the Americas.

Similarly, Ferdinand Magellan's expedition to circumnavigate the globe demonstrated unparalleled boldness. Undertaken in the early 16th century, Magellan's voyage faced mutinies, harsh weather, and uncharted seas. Although Magellan himself did not survive the journey, his expedition proved that the Earth could be circled by sea, fundamentally altering humanity's understanding of geography and global interconnectedness.

The bold actions of explorers during this era remind us that progress often demands venturing into the unknown. Their willingness to act in the face of uncertainty underscores a universal truth: growth and discovery require stepping beyond the boundaries of the familiar.

Industrial Pioneers: Redefining Progress

While the Age of Discovery expanded geographical horizons, the Industrial Revolution redefined the boundaries of innovation and productivity. Industrial pioneers like James Watt, Eli Whitney, and Andrew Carnegie transformed industries through bold action, laying the groundwork for the modern economy.

James Watt's improvements to the steam engine in the late 18th century exemplify the transformative potential of bold action. Watt recognized that existing steam engines were inefficient, limiting their practical applications. Despite limited resources and numerous technical challenges, he pursued his vision of a more efficient engine, ultimately developing a design that revolutionized manufacturing, transportation, and agriculture. Watt's steam engine became a cornerstone of the Industrial Revolution, demonstrating how bold action can catalyze societal change.

Similarly, Eli Whitney's invention of the cotton gin in 1793 showcased the power of innovation to address pressing challenges. Faced with the labor-intensive process of separating cotton fibers from seeds, Whitney devised a machine that dramatically increased efficiency. Although his invention faced legal disputes and resistance from established interests, it transformed the textile industry and reshaped economies across the world.

Andrew Carnegie's journey from an impoverished immigrant to one of the wealthiest industrialists of the 19th century highlights the entrepreneurial boldness of the era. Carnegie's investments in steel production, coupled with his willingness to embrace new technologies and business strategies, revolutionized infrastructure development in the United States. His story illustrates how bold action, driven by vision and determination, can create lasting impact.

The Philosophical Foundations of Bold Action

The bold actions of explorers and industrial pioneers were not random or impulsive—they were guided by a philosophical commitment to progress and possibility. This mindset, rooted in the belief that action is a pathway to discovery, resonates across cultures and eras.

Philosopher John Stuart Mill argued that progress depends on the willingness to challenge norms and pursue innovation. "Genius can only breathe freely in an atmosphere of freedom," Mill wrote, emphasizing the importance of acting boldly to explore new ideas. This perspective highlights the interplay between courage and creativity, suggesting that bold action is not merely a response to external challenges but a reflection of internal curiosity and ambition.

Similarly, the Japanese concept of *kaizen*, or continuous improvement, underscores the importance of taking incremental but purposeful action. While boldness often evokes images of grand gestures, *kaizen* reminds us that bold action can also manifest in consistent, deliberate steps toward a larger goal.

Lessons for Modern Boldness

The stories of historical explorers and industrial pioneers offer valuable lessons for contemporary readers seeking to embrace bold action in their own lives. First, they remind us that uncertainty is an inherent part of progress. The explorers who set sail without clear maps and the inventors who pursued untested ideas faced risks that often seemed insurmountable. Yet, their willingness to act transformed challenges into opportunities for discovery and innovation.

Second, these stories highlight the importance of perseverance. Whether it was Magellan navigating treacherous waters or Watt refining his steam engine, bold action requires resilience in the face of setbacks. This resilience is not just about enduring hardship but about learning from it and adapting strategies to overcome obstacles.

Finally, the actions of historical pioneers underscore the power of vision. Boldness is not about acting recklessly but about pursuing a purpose that inspires and motivates. By aligning actions with a clear sense of purpose, we can channel our energy toward meaningful goals, creating momentum that drives progress.

The Enduring Impact of Bold Action

The bold actions of the past continue to shape our world, reminding us of the transformative power of courage and initiative. From the explorers who mapped the globe to the industrialists who built modern economies, these individuals demonstrate that progress is born not from hesitation but from movement. Their stories challenge us to embrace boldness in our own lives, stepping into the unknown with the confidence that action creates possibilities.

In the face of uncertainty, bold action is not just a tool for survival—it is a catalyst for reinvention. By learning from the examples of history, we can cultivate the mindset and strategies needed to act with purpose, resilience, and creativity. As we chart our own paths forward, the legacy of bold action serves as both a guide and an inspiration, reminding us that the future belongs to those who dare to move.

Momentum-Building Strategies

Momentum is the lifeblood of progress. It transforms isolated actions into sustained movement, allowing us to build on small successes and overcome obstacles with increasing ease. Yet momentum doesn't arise by chance—it must be cultivated through deliberate strategies and thoughtful effort. Whether we are pursuing personal goals, navigating professional challenges, or leading others toward a collective vision, understanding how to create and sustain momentum is essential for meaningful reinvention.

The Power of Starting Small

Building momentum often begins with small, manageable steps. When a goal feels overwhelming, even the simplest action can break the cycle of inertia and create a sense of forward movement. The key is to focus on progress, not perfection.

Consider the example of Ernest Shackleton, the legendary Antarctic explorer. When Shackleton's ship, the *Endurance*, became trapped in ice during an expedition, he faced a seemingly impossible challenge: leading his crew of 27 men to safety across hundreds of miles of treacherous terrain. Shackleton's approach was rooted in breaking the journey into smaller, attainable goals. Each day, he focused on the next immediate step—whether it was setting up camp, rationing supplies, or navigating ice flows.

This strategy not only kept the crew physically moving but also maintained their morale. By achieving small victories along the way, Shackleton created a sense of momentum that ultimately carried them through their harrowing ordeal. His leadership exemplifies how breaking a daunting task into smaller steps can generate the energy and focus needed to sustain progress.

For modern readers, the principle is the same. Whether writing a book, launching a business, or embarking on a fitness journey, starting small provides the foundation for larger achievements. Each small success reinforces confidence and motivation, creating a ripple effect that propels us forward.

Harnessing the Psychology of Momentum

Momentum is not just a physical phenomenon—it is deeply psychological. When we see progress, no matter how incremental, our brains release dopamine, a neurotransmitter associated with reward and motivation. This chemical response reinforces our efforts, making us more likely to continue taking action.

The concept of "keystone habits," popularized by Charles Duhigg in *The Power of Habit*, highlights this dynamic. Keystone habits are small, positive routines that create a cascading effect, influencing other areas of our lives. For example, committing to a daily morning walk might lead to better time management, healthier eating, and increased productivity. These interconnected changes build momentum, amplifying the impact of the initial habit.

By identifying and implementing keystone habits, we can create a psychological environment that supports sustained action. The key is to choose habits that align with our goals and values, ensuring that each action contributes to a larger sense of purpose.

The Role of Planning and Preparation

While action is the engine of momentum, planning and preparation provide the fuel. Clear, actionable plans help us focus our efforts, reduce decision fatigue, and anticipate potential challenges. The act of planning itself can generate momentum by clarifying our goals and breaking them into manageable steps.

One striking example comes from the Apollo 11 mission, which landed humans on the moon in 1969. The success of this historic achievement was not the result of a single bold action but of meticulous planning and preparation over a decade. Engineers, scientists, and astronauts worked tirelessly to solve complex problems, testing each component of the mission through countless simulations and prototypes.

This methodical approach ensured that when the moment of action arrived, the team could execute with confidence and precision. For individuals and teams alike, the lesson is clear: preparation amplifies the effectiveness of action, allowing us to build momentum with purpose and direction.

Overcoming Setbacks

Momentum is rarely a straight line. Setbacks, obstacles, and unexpected challenges are inevitable parts of any journey. The ability to maintain momentum in the face of adversity requires resilience, adaptability, and a willingness to learn from failure.

The story of Walt Disney illustrates this principle. Before creating the iconic Disney empire, Walt faced numerous failures, including the bankruptcy of his first animation studio. Yet, instead of giving up, he used each setback as an opportunity to refine his vision and improve his craft. When his early character, Oswald the Lucky Rabbit, was taken from him due to a contractual dispute, Walt channeled his frustration into creating Mickey Mouse, a character that would become the cornerstone of his legacy.

Disney's resilience demonstrates that setbacks are not the end of momentum—they are opportunities to recalibrate and continue moving forward. By viewing challenges as learning experiences rather than roadblocks, we can maintain our focus and keep building momentum toward our goals.

The Importance of Rest and Reflection

While momentum is about movement, it is equally important to incorporate rest and reflection into the process. Just as a car needs fuel and maintenance to keep running, our minds and bodies require time to recharge. Rest is not a break from progress—it is a vital part of sustaining it.

Reflection, too, plays a critical role in maintaining momentum. By regularly evaluating our progress, we can identify what is working, adjust our strategies, and celebrate our achievements. This practice not only reinforces motivation but also ensures that our actions remain aligned with our overarching goals.

One illustrative example comes from the world of sports. Elite athletes, such as marathon runners, often follow a cycle of intense training followed by periods of rest and recovery. This approach prevents burnout, reduces the risk of injury, and allows the body to adapt and improve. For those pursuing personal or professional goals, adopting a similar rhythm of effort and rest can enhance both performance and well-being.

Building a Support System

Momentum is easier to sustain when we are surrounded by supportive people who encourage our efforts and hold us accountable. Whether it's a mentor, a friend, or a community of like-minded individuals, a strong support system provides the encouragement and perspective needed to stay on track.

Consider the role of the Lunar Society, an 18th-century group of innovators and thinkers who supported one another in advancing scientific and industrial progress. Members like James Watt, Joseph Priestley, and Erasmus Darwin met regularly to exchange ideas, collaborate on projects, and inspire one another. Their collective momentum fueled breakthroughs that shaped the Industrial Revolution.

In our own lives, building a network of supportive relationships can create a similar dynamic. By sharing our goals and challenges with others, we gain access to fresh ideas, constructive feedback, and the motivation to keep moving forward.

The Path Forward

Momentum is not a single act—it is a continuous process of starting, learning, and growing. By focusing on small, achievable steps, harnessing the psychology of progress, and preparing thoughtfully, we can build and sustain the energy needed for meaningful change. Along the way, setbacks and rest are not interruptions but integral parts of the journey, providing opportunities to learn, recharge, and realign.

The strategies for building momentum are as diverse as the challenges we face, but their essence is universal: action creates energy, and energy sustains progress. By committing to the process, we transform isolated efforts into a powerful force for reinvention. As we move forward, each step builds on the last, propelling us toward a future defined by growth, resilience, and achievement.

CHAPTER 4: EMBRACING FAILURE – LESSONS FROM THE GREATEST SETBACKS

Redefining Failure

Failure, a word often cloaked in negativity, is an unavoidable aspect of the human experience. It stirs emotions of frustration, regret, and even shame, making it a phenomenon many strive to avoid at all costs. Yet, history and human progress reveal a counterintuitive truth: failure is not a roadblock but a stepping stone. When reframed, it becomes a powerful learning tool, offering insights, resilience, and the foundation for future success. Redefining failure is not about diminishing its challenges but recognizing its value as an essential component of growth and reinvention.

Edison's "Failed" Lightbulbs: A Masterclass in Persistence

Few figures embody the transformative potential of failure as vividly as Thomas Edison. His journey to invent the electric lightbulb is often celebrated, but it was not a straightforward path. Edison's pursuit of a functional lightbulb involved thousands of experiments and countless setbacks. Each failure was not merely a misstep but an opportunity to learn what didn't work, narrowing the possibilities and bringing him closer to the solution.

When questioned about his repeated failures, Edison's perspective was strikingly optimistic. "I have not failed," he famously remarked. "I've just found 10,000 ways that won't work." This mindset reframed failure as a natural and necessary part of the creative process. For Edison, each failed experiment was a piece of the puzzle, a crucial step in the journey toward his groundbreaking invention.

Edison's approach underscores a vital lesson: failure is not the antithesis of success but a prerequisite for it. By viewing setbacks as learning opportunities rather than dead ends, we cultivate the resilience and curiosity needed to achieve our goals. Edison's story reminds us that the path to success is rarely linear; it is a winding road paved with lessons gleaned from failure.

Marie Curie's Scientific Setbacks

Marie Curie, one of history's most revered scientists, offers another compelling example of failure's transformative power. As a pioneer in the study of radioactivity, Curie faced significant challenges, both scientific and personal. Her experiments often led to unexpected results or inconclusive data, requiring repeated trials and refinements.

Curie's persistence in the face of failure was remarkable. Her groundbreaking discovery of the elements polonium and radium came after years of painstaking research, much of which involved sifting through tons of pitchblende ore to isolate trace amounts of radioactive material. The process was labor-intensive and fraught with setbacks, but Curie's determination never wavered.

Curie's story reveals that failure is an inherent part of innovation. Scientific discovery, by its nature, is a process of trial and error. Each "failure" contributes to the broader understanding of a problem, bringing researchers closer to a breakthrough. For Curie, the lessons learned from her setbacks not only advanced her field but also solidified her legacy as one of the greatest scientists of all time.

The Philosophy of Failure

Beyond historical examples, the concept of failure has been explored extensively in philosophy and psychology. Thinkers like Friedrich Nietzsche and Carl Jung recognized failure as an integral aspect of human development. Nietzsche's concept of the *Übermensch*, or "overman," emphasizes the idea that struggle and failure are necessary for growth and self-overcoming. Similarly, Jung viewed setbacks as opportunities for individuation, the process of becoming one's true self.

Modern psychology supports these philosophical insights. Research on resilience and growth mindset, popularized by psychologist Carol Dweck, highlights the importance of viewing failure as a learning opportunity. A growth mindset, characterized by the belief that abilities and intelligence can be developed through effort and learning, transforms the experience of failure. Instead of seeing it as a reflection of inherent limitations, individuals with a growth mindset perceive failure as a challenge to overcome and an opportunity to improve.

This perspective is liberating. By redefining failure as a natural part of the learning process, we remove the stigma and fear that often accompany it. Instead of avoiding failure, we can embrace it as a catalyst for growth and reinvention.

Practical Lessons from Failure

The stories of Edison and Curie, along with the philosophical and psychological insights, offer practical guidance for reframing failure in our own lives. The first step is to shift our perspective. Instead of asking, "What went wrong?" we can ask, "What can I learn from this?" This subtle but powerful shift transforms failure from a source of shame into an opportunity for discovery.

Another key lesson is the importance of resilience. Failure can be disheartening, but it is not a final verdict. Edison's persistence and Curie's dedication demonstrate that success often lies just beyond the point where many would give up. By cultivating resilience, we can endure setbacks and continue moving toward our goals.

Finally, embracing failure requires a willingness

to take risks. As psychologist Brené Brown observes, "There is no innovation and creativity without failure. Period." To achieve meaningful progress, we must step outside our comfort zones, accepting the possibility of failure as the price of growth.

The Transformative Power of Failure

Redefining failure is not about romanticizing setbacks or ignoring their challenges. It is about recognizing that failure is an inevitable and valuable part of any meaningful endeavor. By embracing failure as a teacher, we unlock its potential to guide us toward greater understanding, resilience, and success.

The stories of Edison and Curie remind us that the road to achievement is paved with lessons learned from failure. Their journeys, marked by persistence and discovery, challenge us to view our own setbacks not as barriers but as stepping stones. By reframing failure, we transform it from a source of fear into a catalyst for reinvention, empowering us to navigate life's challenges with courage and curiosity.

In the words of Samuel Beckett, "Ever tried. Ever failed. No matter. Try again. Fail again. Fail better." These words encapsulate the essence of progress—an iterative process fueled by the lessons we glean from each stumble. Failure, far from being the end, is the beginning of transformation. It is the doorway through which we step into our potential, armed with the wisdom that only failure can provide.

The Resilience of Great Minds

Resilience is the quiet force behind the world's most transformative achievements. It is the ability to endure setbacks, confront failure, and persist in the face of adversity. While success often steals the spotlight, resilience is the story behind the story—a narrative of determination, adaptability, and the refusal to give up. Great minds throughout history have demonstrated this quality, turning repeated failures into stepping stones toward monumental achievements. One of the most compelling examples of resilience is Abraham Lincoln's journey to the presidency, a story that epitomizes the power of perseverance.

Abraham Lincoln: From Defeat to Destiny

Abraham Lincoln, often regarded as one of America's greatest presidents, is celebrated for his leadership during the Civil War and his commitment to ending slavery. Yet, before achieving these historic milestones, Lincoln faced a series of personal and professional failures that would have deterred many. His path to the presidency was marked by repeated losses, setbacks, and hardships, each testing his resolve and fortifying his character.

Born into poverty in 1809, Lincoln's early life was shaped by struggle. He endured the loss of his mother at a young age, limited formal education, and financial instability. As he entered adulthood, Lincoln's challenges only grew. His first business venture, a general store, failed, leaving him deeply in debt. Determined to move forward, he turned to politics, only to face a string of electoral defeats.

Lincoln's persistence, however, never wavered. He continued to pursue his goals despite public rejections and personal tragedies, including the death of his beloved son Edward and ongoing struggles with depression. Each failure served as a crucible, refining his sense of purpose and deepening his understanding of leadership. When he finally won the presidency in 1860, Lincoln brought with him the resilience forged through decades of adversity.

As president, Lincoln's trials were far from over. He navigated the nation through its darkest hours, grappling with the immense pressures of the Civil War, political opposition, and the moral imperative to abolish slavery. Yet, his resilience remained unshaken. Lincoln's ability to persevere, learn from his failures, and maintain a steady vision for the future ultimately transformed the course of American history.

The Role of Resilience in Innovation

Resilience is not confined to the realm of politics—it is equally essential in innovation, where failure is often a prerequisite for progress. One striking example comes from the life of Dr. Robert Goddard, the pioneer of modern rocketry. In the early 20th century, Goddard faced widespread skepticism and ridicule for his vision of space exploration. His early experiments frequently ended in failure, with rockets that exploded, misfired, or failed to launch altogether.

Despite these setbacks, Goddard remained resolute. He meticulously analyzed each failure, refining his designs and pushing the boundaries of what was technologically possible. Over time, his efforts bore fruit, laying the groundwork for the space age and earning him recognition as the father of modern rocketry. Goddard's resilience in the face of failure highlights the critical role of persistence in achieving breakthroughs.

Resilience as a Mindset

The resilience demonstrated by Lincoln, Goddard, and countless others is not simply a reaction to failure—it is a mindset. It involves viewing setbacks not as endpoints but as opportunities for growth and reinvention. This perspective is echoed in the philosophy of stoicism, which emphasizes the importance of accepting challenges with equanimity and focusing on what lies within our control.

Marcus Aurelius, the Roman emperor and stoic philosopher, wrote extensively about resilience in his *Meditations*. He urged readers to embrace difficulties as part of life's natural order, framing adversity as an opportunity to cultivate inner strength. "The impediment to action advances action," he observed. "What stands in the way becomes the way." This stoic principle encourages us to see obstacles not as barriers but as integral components of the path forward.

Modern psychology reinforces this philosophy through the concept of "post-traumatic growth," which suggests that individuals can experience significant personal development as a result of adversity. Studies have shown that those who cultivate resilience often emerge from challenges with greater clarity, purpose, and self-awareness.

The Practical Application of Resilience

While the resilience of historical figures like Lincoln and Goddard may seem extraordinary, their qualities are not beyond reach. Resilience is a skill that can be nurtured through intentional practices and a commitment to growth. One of the most effective ways to build resilience is through reflection—examining failures to identify lessons and areas for improvement.

Another key strategy is reframing adversity. By shifting our perspective to view setbacks as temporary and surmountable, we reduce their emotional impact and regain a sense of agency. For example, rather than interpreting a failed project as evidence of inadequacy, we can frame it as a valuable learning experience that enhances our future efforts.

Support systems also play a vital role in fostering resilience. Surrounding ourselves with mentors, friends, and colleagues who offer encouragement and constructive feedback creates an environment where resilience can thrive. Abraham Lincoln's own resilience was bolstered by a network of trusted advisors and allies, whose support helped him navigate the immense challenges of his presidency.

Resilience in Action

The stories of Lincoln and Goddard, along with the philosophical and psychological insights on resilience, offer a powerful blueprint for overcoming failure. Resilience does not eliminate challenges—it empowers us to confront them with courage and determination. By cultivating this mindset, we transform setbacks into stepping stones, building the strength needed to achieve our goals.

In the face of failure, resilience reminds us that progress is not a straight line. It is a journey marked by twists, turns, and occasional detours. Yet, with each step forward, we grow stronger, wiser, and more prepared to navigate the path ahead. As Lincoln's life demonstrates, resilience is not the absence of failure—it is the ability to rise again, turning even the greatest setbacks into opportunities for reinvention.

Cultural Attitudes Toward Failure

Failure is a universal experience, yet how we perceive and respond to it is deeply influenced by culture. Across the globe, societies have developed distinct attitudes toward failure, shaping how individuals approach challenges, setbacks, and resilience. While some cultures view failure as a natural and necessary part of growth, others stigmatize it, discouraging risk-taking and innovation. By examining these cultural perspectives, we can gain valuable insights into how attitudes toward failure influence personal development and societal progress.

Eastern Philosophies: Embracing Imperfection and Growth

In many Eastern cultures, failure is often viewed through the lens of growth and interconnectedness, emphasizing its role in personal and communal development. Philosophical traditions such as Buddhism and Confucianism encourage acceptance of imperfection and the continuous pursuit of self-improvement.

Buddhism, for instance, teaches that suffering and setbacks are intrinsic to life. The Four Noble Truths, a cornerstone of Buddhist philosophy, highlight that dissatisfaction and struggle are universal, and that liberation from suffering comes through self-awareness and mindful action. This perspective reframes failure as an opportunity to cultivate wisdom and compassion, rather than a reflection of personal inadequacy.

Similarly, the Japanese concept of *wabi-sabi* finds beauty in imperfection and impermanence.

Rooted in Zen philosophy, *wabi-sabi* encourages individuals to embrace flaws as part of the human experience. This outlook fosters resilience by normalizing setbacks and viewing them as essential components of growth. The art of kintsugi, where broken pottery is repaired with gold, visually embodies this philosophy, symbolizing that flaws and failures can enhance, rather than diminish, value.

These Eastern perspectives challenge the notion of failure as something to be feared or avoided. Instead, they position it as a vital step on the path to self-awareness and fulfillment, offering a model for resilience that emphasizes acceptance and transformation.

Western Philosophies: The Duality of Failure

Western attitudes toward failure are more diverse, reflecting the interplay of individualism, ambition, and societal expectations. While some Western traditions celebrate failure as a precursor to success, others attach stigma to setbacks, creating a paradoxical relationship with resilience.

In the United States, the culture of entrepreneurship has fostered a relatively positive view of failure. The mantra "fail fast, fail often" is a common refrain in Silicon Valley, reflecting the belief that innovation thrives on experimentation and learning from mistakes. Iconic entrepreneurs like Steve Jobs and Elon Musk have popularized this ethos, demonstrating that failure is not only survivable but often essential for achieving breakthroughs.

At the same time, Western societies, particularly in Europe, have historically emphasized achievement and perfection. In cultures where academic and professional success are highly valued, failure can carry a significant social stigma. This pressure to avoid failure at all costs can lead to risk aversion, stifling creativity and resilience.

Philosophical traditions in the West offer a nuanced perspective on failure. Ancient Greek philosophers like Aristotle and Socrates viewed failure as a necessary aspect of ethical growth and the pursuit of knowledge. Socrates, for example, embraced intellectual humility, arguing that recognizing one's ignorance was the first step toward wisdom. Similarly, existentialist thinkers like Jean-Paul Sartre and Simone de Beauvoir emphasized the importance of embracing life's uncertainties, including failure, as a means of creating meaning and authenticity.

These contrasting Western attitudes highlight the complexity of failure's role in shaping resilience. While some aspects of Western culture celebrate failure as a catalyst for innovation, others perpetuate fear of failure, underscoring the need for a balanced perspective.

Collective vs. Individual Perspectives on Failure

Cultural attitudes toward failure also differ based on whether a society prioritizes collectivism or individualism. In collectivist cultures, such as those found in many Asian and African countries, failure is often viewed in the context of its impact on the group. The emphasis on harmony and communal well-being can lead to a more cautious approach to risk-taking, as individual failures may be perceived as reflecting on the larger community.

For example, in traditional Chinese culture, the concept of *mianzi* (face) underscores the importance of maintaining dignity and reputation. Fear of losing face can discourage individuals from taking risks or acknowledging mistakes, as failure is seen as a potential source of shame for both the individual and their family or organization. However, this same emphasis on collective well-being can also foster resilience through communal support and shared responsibility for overcoming setbacks.

In contrast, individualist cultures, such as those prevalent in the United States and Western Europe, often frame failure as a personal experience. This perspective can empower individuals to take bold risks and learn from their mistakes, as personal growth is highly valued. However, it can also create a sense of isolation, as individuals may feel solely responsible for their failures without the buffering support of a collective framework.

Learning from Diverse Perspectives

The varied cultural attitudes toward failure offer valuable lessons for building resilience. Eastern philosophies remind us of the importance of acceptance and the beauty of imperfection, encouraging us to view failure as a natural and enriching part of life. Western traditions, particularly in entrepreneurial contexts, highlight the transformative potential of bold risk-taking and iterative learning.

By integrating these perspectives, we can cultivate a more balanced approach to failure—one that combines the humility and acceptance of Eastern thought with the ambition and innovation of Western culture. This holistic mindset allows us to embrace failure as both a personal journey and a communal opportunity, fostering resilience and growth on multiple levels.

Practical Applications for Resilience

Cultural insights into failure can inform practical strategies for navigating setbacks in our own lives. For instance, adopting a *wabi-sabi* mindset can help us reframe personal failures as opportunities for reinvention. Embracing the entrepreneurial mantra of "fail fast, fail often" can encourage experimentation and reduce the fear of making mistakes. At the same time, drawing on collectivist values can remind us of the importance of seeking support and collaboration during challenging times.

These strategies demonstrate that resilience is not a fixed trait but a dynamic skill that can be cultivated through intentional practice. By learning from diverse cultural perspectives, we gain the tools to confront failure with grace, curiosity, and determination, transforming setbacks into stepping stones for growth.

A Global Perspective on Resilience

Failure is not confined by borders, and neither is resilience. By examining cultural attitudes toward failure, we uncover a tapestry of wisdom that enriches our understanding of human potential. Whether we draw inspiration from Eastern philosophies of imperfection, Western celebrations of risk, or the communal resilience of collectivist societies, we find that failure is not an endpoint but a beginning.

In a world that often equates failure with inadequacy, embracing diverse perspectives empowers us to redefine our relationship with setbacks. It reminds us that failure, far from being a mark of weakness, is a universal experience that unites us across cultures and generations. By approaching failure with open minds and open hearts, we unlock its transformative power, paving the way for resilience, reinvention, and renewal.

Learning from Mistakes

Mistakes are inevitable, yet they hold transformative potential when approached with the right mindset. Learning from failure is not a passive process—it requires deliberate effort to analyze setbacks, extract insights, and translate lessons into actionable steps. Throughout history, individuals and organizations that have embraced this approach have not only rebounded from failure but also achieved remarkable success. By adopting practical strategies for learning from mistakes, we can transform setbacks into stepping stones for growth and reinvention.

The Anatomy of a Mistake

Understanding failure begins with acknowledging its complexity. Mistakes can stem from a range of factors, including insufficient preparation, external circumstances, or flawed execution. While the initial reaction to failure is often emotional—frustration, disappointment, or regret—these feelings can obscure the valuable lessons embedded within the experience. To learn from failure, we must shift our perspective, viewing mistakes not as personal shortcomings but as opportunities for growth.

The Apollo 13 mission provides a compelling example of this principle in action. When an oxygen tank exploded during the mission, threatening the lives of the astronauts on board, NASA's team faced a seemingly insurmountable challenge. Yet, instead of succumbing to panic or blame, the team focused on problem-solving, analyzing the situation with precision and ingenuity. Their ability to learn from the unfolding crisis not only saved the crew but also contributed to the development of safer spacecraft systems in the future.

The Apollo 13 story underscores the importance of analyzing mistakes with clarity and objectivity. By focusing on solutions rather than dwelling on the setback itself, we create the conditions for meaningful learning and improvement.

Steps to Analyze Failure

To extract valuable lessons from mistakes, it is essential to adopt a structured approach to analysis. The first step is reflection—taking the time to revisit the experience and identify what went wrong. This process involves asking questions such as:

- *What were my initial goals, and how did they align with my actions?*

- *What external factors influenced the outcome?*

- *What decisions or assumptions contributed to the mistake?*

This reflective process requires honesty and self-compassion. Blame and defensiveness hinder learning, while curiosity and openness create the space for growth.

The next step is to identify patterns and recurring themes. Are there habits or behaviors that consistently lead to setbacks? Recognizing these patterns allows us to address root causes rather than surface-level symptoms. For example, a recurring tendency to overcommit may point to the need for better time management, while repeated miscommunications might highlight the importance of clearer collaboration strategies.

Finally, it is essential to translate insights into actionable changes. This step transforms abstract lessons into concrete improvements, ensuring that the knowledge gained from failure is integrated into future efforts.

Turning Setbacks into Stepping Stones

One of the most powerful aspects of failure is its ability to catalyze growth. When approached with intention, setbacks can provide the insights and motivation needed to achieve greater success.

The story of Sara Blakely, the founder of Spanx, illustrates this principle beautifully. Before launching her groundbreaking brand, Blakely faced numerous rejections and setbacks in her career. A failed attempt at law school and a string of unsatisfying jobs might have discouraged her, but instead, they fueled her determination to create something meaningful. Blakely credits her ability to learn from failure as a key factor in her success, emphasizing the importance of resilience and adaptability.

Blakely's journey highlights the transformative power of reframing failure. By viewing setbacks as opportunities to refine her vision and strategy, she was able to turn obstacles into advantages. This mindset, which she describes as "failing forward," is a cornerstone of innovation and reinvention.

Practical Techniques for Learning from Mistakes

To turn setbacks into stepping stones, consider adopting practical techniques that encourage learning and growth. One effective approach is the "pre-mortem," a proactive strategy that involves imagining potential failures before they occur. By anticipating challenges and devising contingency plans, individuals and teams can reduce the likelihood of mistakes and improve their ability to respond when setbacks arise.

Another valuable technique is the "after-action review," commonly used in military and organizational settings. This process involves analyzing a project or task after its completion, identifying successes, failures, and areas for improvement. By incorporating after-action reviews into routine practice, we create a culture of continuous learning and adaptation.

Additionally, seeking feedback from others can provide fresh perspectives and uncover blind spots. Mentors, colleagues, and trusted friends can offer valuable insights that deepen our understanding of mistakes and illuminate paths forward.

The Role of Mindset in Learning

Learning from failure requires not only practical techniques but also a supportive mindset. A growth mindset, as described by psychologist Carol Dweck, is essential for embracing setbacks as opportunities for development. This mindset involves believing that abilities and intelligence can be cultivated through effort and learning, rather than being fixed traits.

One powerful way to cultivate a growth mindset is through the practice of self-compassion. By treating ourselves with kindness and understanding in the face of failure, we create an environment where learning can flourish. Research shows that self-compassion enhances resilience, motivation, and overall well-being, making it a vital component of the learning process.

The Gift of Failure

When approached with intention and humility, failure becomes a gift—a teacher that guides us toward greater wisdom and strength. The lessons we extract from mistakes are not merely intellectual insights but profound opportunities for transformation. They shape our character, refine our goals, and deepen our understanding of what it means to grow.

The stories of Apollo 13, Sara Blakely, and countless others remind us that failure is not the end of the road but a fork in the path. By choosing to learn from our mistakes, we transform setbacks into stepping stones, paving the way for resilience, reinvention, and success.

In the words of Maya Angelou, "You may encounter many defeats, but you must not be defeated." Failure, when embraced with courage and curiosity, becomes a powerful ally, reminding us of our capacity to rise, learn, and thrive. With each mistake, we gain the tools to navigate life's challenges and move closer to the fulfillment of our potential.

CHAPTER 5: FLEXIBILITY OVER RIGIDITY – THE STRENGTH IN ADAPTABILITY

Why Adaptability Wins

The ability to adapt has long been recognized as a cornerstone of survival and success. In a world marked by constant change and unpredictability, flexibility often trumps rigidity. Those who can pivot, adjust, and evolve in response to shifting circumstances not only endure but thrive. Adaptability is more than a trait—it is a mindset, a strategy, and a measure of resilience. From the natural world to human history, countless examples underscore why adaptability consistently outperforms inflexibility.

Darwin's Theory of Evolution: The Power of Adaptation

Charles Darwin's theory of evolution by natural selection is one of the most profound illustrations of adaptability's supremacy. In his groundbreaking work, *On the Origin of Species*, Darwin observed that survival is not determined by strength or intelligence alone but by the ability to adapt to one's environment. Species that could modify their behaviors, diets, or habitats in response to changing conditions were more likely to endure, while those that remained static faced extinction.

Consider the Galápagos finches, a species Darwin studied extensively. These birds evolved diverse beak shapes and sizes, each suited to the specific food sources available on their respective islands. When environmental conditions shifted, such as a change in climate or the availability of seeds, the finches' adaptability allowed them to survive and even thrive.

Darwin's observations reveal a timeless truth: adaptability is not a luxury but a necessity. In the natural world, rigidity often leads to stagnation and decline, while flexibility enables growth and innovation. This principle applies equally to human endeavors, where the ability to adapt can determine the difference between success and failure.

Agile Military Strategies: Flexibility in Action

History is replete with examples of military leaders who embraced adaptability to achieve victory against formidable odds. One of the most striking illustrations comes from World War II, when the Allies employed agile strategies to counter the Axis powers' initial advantages.

During the North African Campaign, British General Bernard Montgomery demonstrated the power of adaptability in the Battle of El Alamein. Faced with the challenge of overcoming the formidable German Afrika Korps, Montgomery devised a flexible strategy that combined deception, mobility, and relentless preparation. By adapting his tactics to exploit the enemy's weaknesses and respond to their movements, Montgomery achieved a decisive victory that turned the tide of the war in the Allies' favor.

In contrast, the rigidity of certain Axis strategies, such as Germany's inflexible reliance on Blitzkrieg tactics, ultimately proved to be a liability. As the war progressed, the Allies adapted their defenses and countermeasures, neutralizing the effectiveness of these once-dominant tactics.

The lessons of military history underscore the importance of flexibility in navigating complex and dynamic situations. Adaptability allows leaders to respond to uncertainty with creativity and agility, transforming challenges into opportunities for success.

Flexibility as a Strategic Advantage

The advantages of adaptability extend far beyond survival—they encompass growth, innovation, and resilience. In the business world, companies that embrace flexibility are often better equipped to navigate market disruptions, technological advancements, and changing consumer preferences.

Consider the story of Netflix, a company that has repeatedly demonstrated the power of adaptability. Founded in 1997 as a DVD rental service, Netflix faced a critical juncture in the early 2000s as streaming technology emerged. Rather than clinging to its original business model, the company pivoted to become a streaming platform, revolutionizing the entertainment industry.

Netflix's willingness to adapt did not stop there. As competition intensified, the company began producing its own content, launching original series like *House of Cards* and *Stranger Things*. This strategic flexibility allowed Netflix to stay ahead of its rivals and maintain its position as a market leader.

In contrast, companies that resist change often struggle to remain relevant. Blockbuster, once a dominant player in the home video market, failed to adapt to the rise of streaming and ultimately declared bankruptcy in 2010. The contrast between Netflix and Blockbuster illustrates the critical role of adaptability in achieving long-term success.

Philosophical Insights on Flexibility

The importance of adaptability is not limited to science and strategy—it is also deeply rooted in philosophy. The ancient Chinese text *Tao Te Ching*, attributed to Laozi, emphasizes the strength of flexibility through the metaphor of water. "Nothing in the world is softer and weaker than water," Laozi wrote, "but for attacking the hard and strong, nothing surpasses it." Water's ability to flow around obstacles, take different forms, and persist over time embodies the essence of adaptability.

Similarly, stoic philosophers like Epictetus and Marcus Aurelius emphasized the importance of accepting and responding to change. In his *Meditations*, Marcus Aurelius observed that "the impediment to action advances action. What stands in the way becomes the way." This principle highlights the power of adaptability to transform obstacles into opportunities, enabling individuals to navigate life's uncertainties with resilience and grace.

The Cost of Rigidity

While the benefits of adaptability are clear, the dangers of rigidity are equally instructive. Inflexibility often leads to stagnation, as individuals, organizations, and societies struggle to respond to changing circumstances. History offers numerous cautionary tales of entities that failed to adapt and suffered the consequences.

One notable example is the decline of the Ottoman Empire. Once a dominant global power, the empire's inability to modernize its military, economy, and governance structures left it vulnerable to internal and external pressures. While other nations embraced industrialization and innovation, the Ottoman leadership clung to outdated systems, contributing to the empire's eventual collapse.

The story of the Ottoman Empire serves as a reminder that rigidity can be as much a threat to success as external challenges. In a rapidly changing world, the refusal to adapt often results in missed opportunities and irreversible decline.

The Path Forward

Adaptability is not an innate quality but a skill that can be cultivated through practice and intention. By embracing a mindset of curiosity, openness, and flexibility, we can navigate change with confidence and creativity. The stories of Darwin's finches, agile military strategies, and adaptable companies like Netflix illustrate the transformative power of flexibility, offering valuable lessons for individuals and organizations alike.

In the words of Bruce Lee, "Be water, my friend." Flexibility allows us to flow around obstacles, reshape ourselves in response to challenges, and discover new possibilities. It is a strength that empowers us to thrive amid uncertainty, unlocking our potential to grow, innovate, and succeed.

Stories of Adaptable Leaders

Leadership is as much about responding to change as it is about inspiring others. History and modernity alike reveal that the most impactful leaders share a common trait: adaptability. Whether navigating political turbulence, transforming industries, or redefining societal norms, adaptable leaders demonstrate the ability to pivot, adjust, and innovate in the face of uncertainty. Their stories provide powerful lessons on how flexibility can strengthen leadership and foster resilience.

Theodore Roosevelt: The Quintessential Adaptive Leader

Few leaders embody adaptability as fully as Theodore Roosevelt, the 26th president of the United States. Roosevelt's life was a masterclass in reinvention and resilience, shaped by his ability to adapt to diverse challenges and opportunities. Born into a wealthy family in 1858, young Roosevelt struggled with severe asthma and physical frailty, conditions that could have defined his life. Yet, he resolved to strengthen his body and mind through rigorous exercise and relentless self-discipline, transforming himself into an embodiment of vitality and perseverance.

Roosevelt's adaptability extended far beyond personal growth. His political career, marked by a series of bold pivots, demonstrated his ability to navigate complexity with creativity and courage. As New York City's police commissioner, Roosevelt introduced sweeping reforms to combat corruption, earning both praise and resistance. Later, as assistant secretary of the Navy, he advocated for modernization and readiness, positioning the U.S. Navy as a global force.

Perhaps the most striking example of Roosevelt's adaptability came during his presidency. Faced with rapid industrialization and social upheaval, he championed progressive reforms, including antitrust legislation and conservation initiatives. By balancing the demands of diverse constituencies, Roosevelt demonstrated an uncanny ability to adapt his leadership style to the needs of the moment. His legacy, marked by dynamic problem-solving and a commitment to the greater good, underscores the power of adaptability in leadership.

Modern Business Leaders: Innovators of Adaptation

The business world offers equally compelling examples of adaptable leaders who have transformed industries by embracing change. One such leader is Satya Nadella, the CEO of Microsoft. When Nadella took the helm in 2014, the company was facing stagnation, having struggled to adapt to the rise of mobile computing and cloud technologies. Nadella recognized the need for a cultural and strategic shift, emphasizing collaboration, innovation, and customer-centricity.

Under Nadella's leadership, Microsoft pivoted toward cloud computing, investing heavily in its Azure platform. This shift not only revitalized the company's growth but also positioned Microsoft as a leader in the tech industry's most dynamic sector. Nadella's focus on adaptability extended to the company's culture, fostering a mindset of continuous learning and inclusivity. His ability to align strategy with changing market demands exemplifies the transformative power of flexible leadership.

Similarly, Oprah Winfrey's journey as a media mogul highlights the importance of adaptability in sustaining long-term success. Starting as a local news anchor, Winfrey pivoted to daytime television, creating *The Oprah Winfrey Show*, a platform that blended entertainment with meaningful conversations. Recognizing the shifting media landscape, she later transitioned into producing original content through her network, OWN, and digital platforms. Winfrey's ability to adapt her brand to evolving audience preferences has solidified her position as a cultural icon and business powerhouse.

The Common Threads of Adaptable Leadership

While the contexts of Roosevelt, Nadella, and Winfrey differ, their stories share key commonalities. Adaptable leaders possess a keen awareness of their environment, a willingness to embrace uncertainty, and a commitment to learning and growth. They are not confined by rigid ideologies or fixed strategies but instead remain open to new perspectives and possibilities.

This mindset is echoed in the work of leadership scholar Warren Bennis, who argued that effective leaders are "adaptive capacity builders." According to Bennis, the ability to adapt is rooted in emotional intelligence, curiosity, and a capacity for reflection. By cultivating these qualities, leaders can navigate change with agility and inspire others to do the same.

Adaptability in Crisis

The true test of adaptability often comes during crises, when the ability to pivot can mean the difference between failure and survival. During the COVID-19 pandemic, leaders across industries demonstrated remarkable flexibility in responding to unprecedented challenges. For example, Arne Sorenson, the late CEO of Marriott International, navigated the hospitality industry's sharp downturn with transparency and decisiveness. Recognizing the need for immediate action, Sorenson implemented cost-saving measures while prioritizing employee well-being and long-term recovery.

Similarly, Jacinda Ardern, the prime minister
of New Zealand, gained international recognition for her adaptive leadership during the
pandemic. Ardern's approach combined clear
communication, empathy, and data-driven
decision-making, allowing her government to
respond swiftly to emerging threats. Her ability
to balance compassion with pragmatism exemplifies the strength of adaptable leadership in
times of uncertainty.

Philosophical Reflections on Adaptability

The importance of adaptability in leadership
is not a modern insight—it has been a central
theme in philosophical thought for centuries.
Ancient Chinese philosophy, particularly the
teachings of Laozi in the *Tao Te Ching*, emphasizes the value of flexibility. "A leader is best
when people barely know he exists," Laozi
wrote, "when his work is done, his aim fulfilled,
they will say: we did it ourselves." This wisdom
highlights the subtle strength of adaptable leadership, which empowers others while remaining
attuned to the flow of circumstances.

Similarly, Niccolò Machiavelli, in *The Prince*, argued that successful leaders must balance *virtù* (personal ability) with an awareness of *fortuna* (the unpredictability of circumstances). Machiavelli's insights underscore the need for leaders to anticipate change and adjust their strategies accordingly, reinforcing the timeless value of adaptability.

The Path to Adaptable Leadership

Adaptable leadership is not reserved for the extraordinary—it is a skill that can be cultivated through intentional practice. By embracing a mindset of curiosity, humility, and resilience, leaders can navigate complexity with confidence and creativity. The stories of Theodore Roosevelt, Satya Nadella, and Oprah Winfrey remind us that adaptability is not only a tool for overcoming challenges but also a pathway to innovation, growth, and lasting impact.

As the world continues to evolve, the need for adaptable leaders has never been greater. By learning from the examples of those who have demonstrated this quality, we can inspire ourselves and others to embrace change with courage and vision. In the words of Albert Einstein, "The measure of intelligence is the ability to change." For leaders, this ability is not just a measure of intelligence—it is a measure of greatness.

The Science of Adaptability

Adaptability, while often celebrated as a trait of character or leadership, is deeply rooted in the biology and psychology of the human mind. The ability to adjust to new circumstances, pivot in response to challenges, and embrace the unfamiliar is not simply a learned behavior—it is an intrinsic part of what makes us human. Insights from neuroscience, psychology, and behavioral studies illuminate the mechanisms that underpin adaptability, offering practical lessons for enhancing this vital skill.

Neuroplasticity: The Brain's Capacity for Change

At the heart of adaptability lies the concept of neuroplasticity, the brain's remarkable ability to reorganize itself in response to experience. Neuroplasticity allows neural networks to form new connections, strengthen existing pathways, and even reassign functions to different areas of the brain. This dynamic process enables learning, memory, and recovery from injury, and it is the foundation of our capacity to adapt to change.

One of the most striking examples of neuro-plasticity comes from studies on individuals who have suffered brain injuries. Researchers have found that, over time, undamaged areas of the brain can take over functions previously performed by the injured regions. This ability to rewire underscores the brain's inherent flex-ibility, a quality that extends beyond physical recovery to include emotional and cognitive adaptation.

Neuroplasticity is not limited to extraordinary circumstances—it is a continuous process that occurs throughout life. Every time we learn a new skill, adapt to a different environment, or overcome a challenge, we engage the brain's ca-pacity for change. This biological foundation of adaptability highlights the potential for growth and transformation at any stage of life.

The Role of Stress in Adaptation

While stress is often viewed as a negative force, it plays a crucial role in adaptability. Moderate levels of stress, known as eustress, can enhance focus, problem-solving, and resilience. When faced with a challenge, the brain releases stress hormones like cortisol and adrenaline, which activate the body's fight-or-flight response. This heightened state of arousal sharpens our senses and prepares us to respond effectively to new situations.

However, the relationship between stress and adaptability is not linear. Chronic or over-whelming stress can impair cognitive function, leading to rigidity and reduced flexibility. Neuroscientists have found that prolonged exposure to stress can shrink the prefrontal cortex, the region of the brain responsible for decision-making and emotional regulation, while enlarging the amygdala, which governs fear and anxiety. This imbalance can make it harder to adapt to change, as the brain becomes locked into patterns of reactive rather than proactive behavior.

The key to harnessing stress for adaptability lies

in managing its intensity and duration. Practices like mindfulness, exercise, and social support help regulate the body's stress response, allowing us to stay flexible and resourceful in the face of challenges.

Cognitive Flexibility: The Psychology of Adaptation

Adaptability also hinges on cognitive flexibility, the mental ability to shift perspectives, adjust to new rules, and find alternative solutions to problems. Cognitive flexibility is what allows us to pivot when our plans are disrupted, to see opportunities in setbacks, and to approach challenges with creativity and innovation.

Psychological studies have shown that individuals with high cognitive flexibility are better equipped to navigate uncertainty and complexity. For example, research on problem-solving reveals that people who can generate multiple approaches to a single challenge are more likely to find effective solutions. This ability to "think outside the box" is a hallmark of adaptable minds.

Cognitive flexibility is not a fixed trait—it can be developed through intentional practice. Activities that challenge the brain, such as learning a new language, solving puzzles, or exploring unfamiliar environments, enhance neural plasticity and strengthen the mental agility needed for adaptability. Additionally, cultivating an open mindset—being willing to question assumptions and embrace diverse perspectives—fosters the psychological flexibility that underpins resilience.

The Emotional Dimension of Adaptability

While adaptability involves cognitive and biological processes, it is also deeply emotional. Embracing change often requires confronting fear, uncertainty, and discomfort, emotions that can inhibit flexibility if left unchecked. The ability to regulate emotions, a skill known as emotional intelligence, is therefore a critical component of adaptability.

Emotional intelligence involves recognizing, understanding, and managing our emotions, as well as empathizing with others. Studies have found that individuals with high emotional intelligence are more resilient in the face of change, as they are better able to navigate the emotional turbulence that often accompanies new challenges. For example, a leader who can remain calm and composed during a crisis is more likely to inspire confidence and encourage adaptive thinking within their team.

One way to enhance emotional adaptability is through self-compassion. By treating ourselves with kindness and understanding during times of struggle, we create a supportive inner dialogue that fosters resilience. This practice not only reduces the fear of failure but also encourages a growth-oriented mindset, allowing us to approach change with curiosity rather than resistance.

Behavioral Studies on Adaptability

Behavioral science offers additional insights into the mechanisms of adaptability. Experiments on habit formation, for example, reveal that flexibility often depends on our ability to break old habits and establish new ones. Researchers have found that habits are governed by a loop of cue, routine, and reward—a cycle that can be reshaped through intentional effort.

In one study, participants were asked to adopt a new daily habit, such as drinking water before breakfast or taking a short walk after lunch. Over time, those who approached the task with a mindset of experimentation—willing to tweak their routines and learn from setbacks—were more successful in forming lasting habits. This finding underscores the importance of adaptability not only in responding to external change but also in shaping our internal behaviors.

The Interplay of Biology and Psychology

The science of adaptability reveals a dynamic interplay between biology and psychology. Our brains and bodies are wired to respond to change, yet how we interpret and engage with those responses determines our capacity for growth. By understanding the mechanisms of neuroplasticity, cognitive flexibility, and emotional intelligence, we can cultivate the adaptability needed to navigate life's complexities.

Ultimately, the science of adaptability affirms a hopeful truth: we are not bound by our circumstances or limitations. Through intentional practice and self-awareness, we can harness the natural resilience of our minds and bodies, transforming challenges into opportunities for reinvention. This scientific foundation enriches our understanding of adaptability, providing a roadmap for navigating change with confidence and creativity.

Cultivating Adaptability

Adaptability is not merely a skill but a mind-set—a way of engaging with the world that embraces change as an opportunity rather than a threat. While some individuals seem naturally more flexible in their thinking and behavior, adaptability is not an innate trait reserved for the few. It is a capability that can be cultivated through intentional effort, practice, and reflection. By fostering adaptability, we empower ourselves to navigate uncertainty, overcome obstacles, and seize new opportunities in both life and work.

The Art of Embracing Change

Cultivating adaptability begins with a fundamental shift in how we perceive change. For many, change is synonymous with disruption and discomfort, triggering resistance and anxiety. However, when we reframe change as a natural and inevitable part of life, we open ourselves to its transformative potential.

One way to embrace change is through the practice of curiosity. By approaching new situations with a sense of wonder and a willingness to learn, we reduce the fear of the unknown and foster a mindset of exploration. The story of Malala Yousafzai, the youngest Nobel laureate, exemplifies this approach. After surviving an attack on her life for advocating girls' education in Pakistan, Malala adapted to her new circumstances by channeling her experiences into a global movement for education and empowerment. Her curiosity about the world and commitment to learning enabled her to turn personal tragedy into a platform for transformative change.

Curiosity is not only a catalyst for adaptability but also a shield against stagnation. By continually seeking new knowledge, perspectives, and experiences, we strengthen our ability to adjust to shifting circumstances and remain open to growth.

Building Resilience Through Flexibility

Resilience and adaptability are closely intertwined. Resilience provides the emotional strength to persevere through challenges, while adaptability offers the tools to adjust our strategies and perspectives. Together, these qualities enable us to navigate life's uncertainties with confidence and grace.

One practical way to build resilience is by developing a growth mindset—a concept popularized by psychologist Carol Dweck. A growth mindset emphasizes the belief that abilities and intelligence can be developed through effort and learning. This perspective encourages us to view setbacks not as failures but as opportunities to grow and improve. For example, a student who struggles with a difficult subject can use a growth mindset to persist, experimenting with new study techniques and seeking support from teachers or peers.

Another key component of resilience is emotional regulation. Adaptable individuals are often skilled at managing their emotions, allowing them to stay calm and composed in the face of adversity. Practices such as mindfulness meditation, deep breathing, and journaling can enhance emotional regulation, providing a foundation for adaptability.

Practical Strategies for Adaptability

While mindset is essential, adaptability also requires actionable strategies that enable us to respond effectively to change. One such strategy is the art of reframing—viewing challenges from a different perspective to uncover hidden opportunities. For example, an unexpected job loss, while initially distressing, might be reframed as a chance to explore new career paths or pursue long-held passions.

Another powerful tool is flexibility in goal-setting. While long-term goals provide direction, it is equally important to remain open to revising them as circumstances evolve. The concept of "multiple pathways" offers a useful framework: rather than committing to a single rigid plan, we can identify several potential routes to achieve our objectives. This approach not only increases our chances of success but also reduces the pressure to adhere to a predefined script.

Experimentation is another hallmark of adaptability. By testing new ideas, approaches, and routines, we cultivate a mindset of innovation and creativity. Thomas Edison, who famously conducted thousands of experiments before inventing the lightbulb, epitomized the value of experimentation. Each attempt, whether successful or not, brought him closer to his ultimate goal, demonstrating that adaptability often involves iterative learning.

Fostering Adaptability in Teams and Organizations

Adaptability is not only a personal skill—it is also a critical component of effective teamwork and organizational success. In today's rapidly changing world, businesses and communities that prioritize adaptability are better equipped to thrive in the face of disruption.

Leaders play a pivotal role in fostering adaptability within their teams. By creating a culture of psychological safety—where individuals feel comfortable expressing ideas, taking risks, and learning from mistakes—leaders encourage innovation and resilience. For example, Google's Project Aristotle identified psychological safety as the most important factor in high-performing teams, highlighting its role in fostering adaptability.

Organizations can also enhance adaptability by embracing agile methodologies. Originally developed in the software industry, agile principles prioritize flexibility, collaboration, and iterative progress. By breaking projects into smaller, manageable stages and regularly reassessing priorities, teams can respond quickly to changing circumstances and deliver value more effectively.

The Role of Open-Mindedness

Open-mindedness is a cornerstone of adaptability, enabling us to consider diverse perspectives, question assumptions, and embrace new ideas. Cultivating open-mindedness involves a commitment to lifelong learning and a willingness to challenge our own beliefs.

Philosopher John Stuart Mill eloquently captured the importance of open-mindedness in his defense of free thought and debate. "The worth of a state," he wrote, "is the worth of the individuals composing it." Mill argued that exposure to diverse viewpoints strengthens our understanding of the world, fostering the flexibility needed to navigate complexity.

In practice, open-mindedness can be cultivated through intentional habits such as reading widely, engaging in respectful dialogue with those who hold different opinions, and seeking feedback from trusted mentors or peers. By remaining open to new information and experiences, we expand our capacity for adaptability.

The Path to Lifelong Adaptability

Cultivating adaptability is a lifelong journey, one that requires self-awareness, intentionality, and a commitment to growth. By embracing change, building resilience, and adopting practical strategies, we empower ourselves to thrive in an ever-changing world.

The stories of individuals like Malala Yousafzai, the principles of agile leadership, and the wisdom of philosophers like John Stuart Mill remind us that adaptability is not a passive response but an active pursuit. It is a skill that enables us to turn challenges into opportunities, uncertainty into innovation, and setbacks into stepping stones.

In the words of Charles Darwin, "It is not the strongest of the species that survive, nor the most intelligent, but the one most responsive to change." Adaptability is the strength that carries us forward, helping us to navigate life's complexities with courage, creativity, and hope.

CHAPTER 6: THE POWER OF REINVENTION – TRANSFORMING IDENTITY AND PURPOSE

The Case for Reinvention

Reinvention is the art of transforming oneself to align with changing circumstances, evolving goals, and newfound purposes. In a world defined by rapid technological advancements, shifting social dynamics, and personal growth, the ability to reinvent oneself is not just a valuable skill—it is essential. Whether prompted by external pressures or internal aspirations, reinvention allows us to break free from outdated roles, embrace new possibilities, and rediscover our potential.

Nelson Mandela: From Prisoner to President

One of the most profound examples of reinvention comes from the life of Nelson Mandela, a man whose transformation reshaped the destiny of a nation. Born into a rural South African community in 1918, Mandela initially pursued a career as a lawyer, using his education to challenge the injustices of apartheid. However, his activism led to his imprisonment in 1962, where he would spend 27 years confined to a cell on Robben Island.

During his imprisonment, Mandela underwent a profound process of reinvention. Stripped of his freedom and separated from his family, he could have succumbed to bitterness and despair. Instead, Mandela chose to transform himself from a defiant activist into a unifying leader. He cultivated empathy and patience, learning the value of negotiation and compromise. These qualities would later define his presidency and the peaceful transition of South Africa from apartheid to democracy.

When Mandela was released in 1990, he emerged not as a broken man but as a statesman ready to lead a divided nation toward reconciliation. His ability to reinvent himself, to adapt his identity and purpose to the demands of a new era, offers a timeless lesson: reinvention is not about abandoning who we are but about becoming who we need to be.

Apple: A Corporate Transformation

Reinvention is not limited to individuals—it is equally vital for organizations. Few companies illustrate this principle as vividly as Apple. In the mid-1990s, Apple was on the brink of collapse, its products struggling to compete with dominant players like Microsoft. The company's rigid adherence to its original vision, combined with a lack of innovation, had left it stagnant and irrelevant.

The turning point came with the return of Steve Jobs in 1997. Jobs recognized that survival required more than incremental improvements — it demanded a complete transformation. He streamlined Apple's product line, cutting underperforming products to focus on innovation. The release of the iMac, followed by groundbreaking devices like the iPod, iPhone, and iPad, marked a dramatic resurgence.

Apple's reinvention extended beyond its products. The company redefined its identity, branding itself not just as a technology provider but as a cultural icon synonymous with creativity and simplicity. This transformation propelled Apple to become one of the most valuable companies in the world, demonstrating that reinvention is not just a response to failure but a pathway to unprecedented success.

The Necessity of Reinvention

The cases of Mandela and Apple underscore a fundamental truth: reinvention is often born of necessity. Whether driven by personal hardship, market pressures, or societal shifts, the need to adapt is a constant in life. Clinging to outdated roles, strategies, or identities can lead to stagnation, while embracing change opens the door to growth and fulfillment.

Reinvention is not an admission of failure—it is an acknowledgment of evolution. Just as nature thrives through adaptation, so too do individuals and organizations flourish when they align their actions with their evolving environments and aspirations. This principle is evident in the natural world, where species that adapt to changing conditions survive and thrive, while those that remain static risk extinction.

Philosophical Perspectives on Reinvention

The concept of reinvention resonates deeply with philosophical traditions that emphasize growth and transformation. The ancient Greek philosopher Heraclitus famously observed, "No man ever steps in the same river twice, for it's not the same river and he's not the same man." This metaphor highlights the inevitability of change and the necessity of adapting to its flow.

Similarly, existentialist thinkers like Jean-Paul Sartre and Simone de Beauvoir argued that individuals have the freedom—and responsibility—to redefine themselves in response to life's challenges. Sartre's concept of "existence precedes essence" suggests that our identities are not fixed but are shaped by our choices and actions. Reinvention, in this view, is an exercise in self-determination, a way of crafting meaning and purpose in an ever-changing world.

Barriers to Reinvention

Despite its benefits, reinvention is not without its challenges. Fear of the unknown, attachment to familiar routines, and the opinions of others often create resistance to change. These barriers can be particularly strong in moments of uncertainty, when the comfort of the status quo seems preferable to the risks of transformation.

Overcoming these barriers requires courage and self-awareness. It involves recognizing that growth often necessitates discomfort and that the rewards of reinvention far outweigh the temporary challenges of transition. As Mandela's story demonstrates, even the most daunting circumstances can serve as a catalyst for profound transformation when approached with resilience and vision.

Practical Applications of Reinvention

Reinvention is not a one-time event—it is an ongoing process of aligning our identity and actions with our evolving goals. This process begins with introspection: identifying what is no longer serving us and envisioning what we want to become. Whether it involves changing careers, pursuing a new passion, or redefining personal values, reinvention requires clarity of purpose and a willingness to take bold steps.

The story of Apple's resurgence offers practical lessons for this journey. By focusing on core strengths, embracing innovation, and letting go of unproductive strategies, the company created a foundation for long-term success. Similarly, individuals can benefit from identifying their unique strengths and leveraging them to pursue new opportunities.

The Transformative Power of Reinvention

Reinvention is more than a response to change—it is a powerful act of creation. It allows us to shed outdated roles, embrace new possibilities, and align our lives with our deepest aspirations. The stories of Mandela, Apple, and countless others remind us that reinvention is not about abandoning who we are but about evolving into who we are meant to be.

In a world where change is the only constant, the ability to reinvent oneself is the ultimate skill. It is a testament to the resilience of the human spirit and the boundless potential for growth and transformation. As we navigate the complexities of modern life, the case for reinvention becomes ever clearer: it is not just a path to success but a journey toward authenticity and fulfillment.

The Emotional Side of Reinvention

Reinvention, though empowering, is often accompanied by a complex web of emotions. Fear of the unknown, self-doubt, and the discomfort of leaving behind familiar identities can make the process daunting. These emotions, while challenging, are a natural part of transformation. By acknowledging and addressing them, we can navigate the emotional terrain of reinvention with greater clarity and confidence, ultimately emerging stronger and more aligned with our true purpose.

The Fear of Letting Go

One of the most pervasive emotions tied to reinvention is fear—specifically, the fear of letting go. Whether it involves leaving a stable job, moving to a new city, or redefining a long-held sense of self, the act of releasing what no longer serves us can feel like stepping into a void. This fear is rooted in uncertainty: What lies ahead? Will I succeed? Will others accept my new identity?

The story of Maya Angelou illustrates the courage it takes to confront this fear. Before becoming an iconic poet and activist, Angelou underwent multiple reinventions, including stints as a singer, actress, and civil rights worker. Each transformation required her to leave behind a familiar chapter of her life and step into un-charted territory. In her memoir, *I Know Why the Caged Bird Sings*, Angelou reflects on the uncer-tainty and vulnerability that accompanied these changes. Yet, she also reveals how embracing the unknown allowed her to discover deeper layers of creativity and purpose.

Angelou's journey reminds us that fear is not a barrier but a bridge—a sign that we are moving beyond our comfort zones and into the realm of possibility. By reframing fear as a natural re-sponse to growth, we can harness it as a source of energy and motivation.

Self-Doubt: The Inner Critic

Self-doubt often emerges during reinvention, as we question our abilities, choices, and worthi-ness. This inner critic can be particularly loud when we face setbacks or when our new identity is met with skepticism from others. Overcoming self-doubt requires both self-awareness and self-compassion.

The psychological concept of "impostor syn-drome" sheds light on this struggle. Coined in the 1970s, impostor syndrome describes the tendency to doubt one's accomplishments and fear being exposed as a fraud, even in the face of evidence to the contrary. This phenomenon is common during periods of reinvention, as we navigate unfamiliar roles and responsibilities.

The key to overcoming self-doubt lies in challenging negative thought patterns and cultivating a growth mindset. This involves recognizing that skills and confidence are developed through practice, not inherent traits. Consider the example of Eleanor Roosevelt, who transformed herself from a shy, hesitant individual into one of the most influential political figures of her time. Roosevelt's ability to push through self-doubt and embrace her evolving identity demonstrates the power of perseverance and self-belief.

The Discomfort of Transformation

Reinvention often involves a period of discomfort, as old routines and habits give way to new ones. This transitional phase can feel disorienting, like shedding an old skin without yet knowing what lies beneath. However, this discomfort is a necessary part of the process—it is the space where growth occurs.

The metaphor of a butterfly's metamorphosis captures this dynamic beautifully. Before it can fly, a caterpillar must undergo a complete transformation within the cocoon, dissolving its old form to create a new one. This process, though uncomfortable and vulnerable, is essential for the emergence of its new identity.

Similarly, embracing the discomfort of reinvention requires patience and trust in the process. Practices such as journaling, meditation, and seeking support from mentors or peers can help us navigate this phase with greater ease.

Techniques for Embracing New Identities

Successfully navigating the emotional challenges of reinvention involves cultivating techniques that foster resilience and self-discovery. One powerful approach is visualization. By imagining our future selves in vivid detail—how we will look, feel, and act in our new roles—we create a mental blueprint that guides our actions. Visualization not only clarifies our goals but also strengthens our belief in their achievability.

Another effective technique is storytelling. Sharing our journey with others, whether through conversations, writing, or creative expression, allows us to process our emotions and solidify our new identities. Stories help us make sense of change, connecting the dots between where we have been and where we are headed.

Finally, embracing a mindset of experimentation can ease the pressure of transformation. Instead of viewing reinvention as a single, definitive act, we can approach it as an ongoing process of trial and error. This perspective encourages us to take small, manageable steps toward our new identities, celebrating progress along the way.

The Role of Community in Reinvention

While reinvention is a deeply personal journey, it is rarely undertaken alone. The support of a community—whether friends, family, mentors, or like-minded peers—can provide invaluable encouragement and perspective. Surrounding ourselves with individuals who believe in our potential helps counteract self-doubt and reinforces our commitment to growth.

The story of Malala Yousafzai illustrates the power of community in navigating transformation. After surviving an attack for advocating girls' education, Malala found strength in her family's unwavering support and the global community that rallied behind her cause. This collective encouragement enabled her to step into a new role as an international activist, transforming her personal adversity into a platform for change.

Reinvention as a Journey, Not a Destination

The emotional challenges of reinvention—fear, self-doubt, discomfort—are not obstacles to be avoided but integral parts of the process. They remind us that growth requires vulnerability and that transformation is not a one-time event but a continuous journey.

By embracing these emotions with courage and compassion, we unlock the power of reinvention to reshape our identities, align with our purpose, and create a life that reflects our true potential. The path may be uncertain, but as countless stories have shown, it is a journey worth taking. In the words of author Anaïs Nin, "Life shrinks or expands in proportion to one's courage." Reinvention invites us to expand — to step into the unknown and discover the boundless possibilities that lie ahead.

Success Stories of Reinvention

Reinvention is a testament to human resilience and creativity, offering a path forward when faced with challenges or the need for transformation. Throughout history, individuals and organizations have demonstrated that the ability to adapt, innovate, and redefine oneself is not only possible but often necessary for survival and success. Their stories serve as powerful examples of what can be achieved when we embrace the courage to reinvent.

Oprah Winfrey: From Local Anchor to Global Icon

Oprah Winfrey's journey epitomizes the power of reinvention. Born into poverty in Mississippi and facing numerous hardships in her early life, Oprah could have been defined by her circumstances. Instead, she used them as a foundation for growth, transforming herself into one of the most influential figures in media and beyond.

Oprah's first reinvention came during her transition from a local news anchor to a daytime talk show host. Early in her career, she struggled to find her voice in traditional news reporting, which often required a detached, neutral tone. Recognizing that this role did not align with her strengths or passions, Oprah took a risk by embracing a more personal and empathetic style on *The Oprah Winfrey Show*. This decision not only redefined her career but also revolutionized the talk show format, blending entertainment with meaningful conversations about life, relationships, and personal growth.

As the media landscape evolved, Oprah continued to reinvent herself. In 2011, she launched the Oprah Winfrey Network (OWN), transitioning from talk show host to network executive. While the network faced initial challenges, Oprah's perseverance and adaptability transformed OWN into a platform for diverse storytelling and inspiration.

Oprah's story highlights the importance of aligning reinvention with one's core values and strengths. Her ability to pivot while staying true to her authentic self underscores the transformative potential of reinvention when guided by purpose.

Netflix vs. Blockbuster: A Tale of Adaptation

While reinvention can lead to extraordinary success, the failure to adapt often results in decline. The contrasting stories of Netflix and Blockbuster provide a compelling case study of how reinvention—or the lack thereof—shapes organizational survival.

In the early 2000s, Blockbuster dominated the home entertainment industry with thousands of retail stores across the United States. At its peak, the company was synonymous with movie rentals, generating billions in revenue. However, Blockbuster's reliance on its brick-and-mortar model left it vulnerable to technological disruption.

Netflix, a small startup at the time, began as a DVD-by-mail service, challenging Blockbuster's traditional model. Recognizing the potential of streaming technology, Netflix pivoted in 2007, investing heavily in digital infrastructure and content licensing. This bold reinvention transformed Netflix into a pioneer of the streaming era, eventually making it a global entertainment giant.

Blockbuster, by contrast, resisted change. Despite having the resources and opportunity to embrace streaming, the company clung to its existing business model, underestimating the speed of technological innovation. By the time Blockbuster attempted to launch its own streaming service, it was too late. The company filed for bankruptcy in 2010, while Netflix continued to soar.

This cautionary tale underscores the importance of anticipating change and acting decisively. Netflix's success was not merely a result of its vision but of its willingness to reinvent itself, even at the risk of disrupting its original business.

Reinvention Across Industries

Reinvention is not limited to media and entertainment—it occurs across industries, reshaping businesses, careers, and communities. One striking example comes from the automotive sector, where companies like Tesla have redefined the landscape of electric vehicles.

When Tesla was founded in 2003, electric cars were seen as impractical and niche products. Through relentless innovation and a willingness to challenge industry norms, Tesla reinvented the concept of electric vehicles, making them desirable and accessible to mainstream consumers. This reinvention extended beyond product design to include advancements in battery technology, software, and renewable energy solutions, positioning Tesla as a leader in sustainable transportation.

Tesla's story illustrates how reinvention can spark broader societal change, inspiring competitors and governments to prioritize sustainability and innovation. By challenging assumptions and embracing bold ideas, Tesla redefined an industry, proving that reinvention is a powerful force for progress.

The Philosophical Roots of Reinvention

The success stories of Oprah, Netflix, and Tesla are underpinned by a philosophical understanding of change as an opportunity for growth. Ancient Chinese philosophy, particularly the teachings of Laozi in the *Tao Te Ching*, emphasizes the importance of embracing transformation. "When I let go of what I am," Laozi wrote, "I become what I might be." This wisdom reminds us that reinvention often requires releasing old identities to make space for new possibilities.

Similarly, existentialist thinkers like Friedrich Nietzsche and Jean-Paul Sartre explored the concept of self-overcoming—the idea that individuals have the capacity to transcend their limitations and create new meanings in their lives. Nietzsche's concept of the "eternal recurrence" challenges us to imagine living our lives over and over, inspiring a commitment to continual reinvention and self-improvement.

These philosophical perspectives resonate with the stories of successful reinvention, illustrating that transformation is not just a practical endeavor but a deeply human aspiration.

Lessons from Reinvention

The common thread running through these stories is the willingness to embrace change, take risks, and learn from failure. Whether through Oprah's alignment with her authentic voice, Netflix's strategic pivot to streaming, or Tesla's redefinition of an industry, reinvention emerges as a process of bold experimentation and unwavering commitment to growth.

For individuals and organizations alike, these examples offer valuable lessons:

- Reinvention begins with self-awareness, recognizing when existing paths no longer align with evolving goals.

- The ability to anticipate and adapt to change is essential for staying relevant and resilient.

- Authenticity and purpose provide a guiding compass, ensuring that reinvention reflects core values rather than fleeting trends.

As we navigate the complexities of modern life,

the stories of those who have successfully reinvented themselves remind us of our own potential for transformation. Reinvention is not merely a response to change—it is an opportunity to redefine what is possible, both for ourselves and for the world around us.

Reinvention Frameworks

Reinvention is a journey of transformation that requires careful planning, reflection, and action. While the process may seem daunting, a structured approach can provide clarity and direction, empowering individuals and organizations to redefine themselves with confidence. Reinvention is not just about change; it is about intentional growth, guided by purpose and aligned with one's evolving identity and goals. By following a practical framework, we can navigate the complexities of reinvention and emerge stronger, more fulfilled, and better prepared for the future.

Step 1: Define Your Purpose and Vision

Every successful reinvention begins with a clear understanding of why change is necessary and what it seeks to achieve. This step involves introspection—examining your values, goals, and aspirations to identify what no longer serves you and what you wish to embrace.

Consider the story of Howard Schultz, the former CEO of Starbucks, who reinvented the company during a period of stagnation in the late 2000s. Schultz began by revisiting Starbucks' core mission: to inspire and nurture the human spirit. Recognizing that the company had drifted from its original values, Schultz spearheaded a transformation that focused on quality, customer experience, and community engagement. This clear sense of purpose guided Starbucks' reinvention, revitalizing its brand and restoring its position as a leader in the coffee industry.

For individuals, defining purpose often involves envisioning the life you want to create. Visualization exercises, journaling, and conversations with trusted mentors can help clarify your vision and establish a compelling "why" for your reinvention.

Step 2: Assess Your Current State

Before embarking on reinvention, it is essential to take stock of your current situation. This includes evaluating your strengths, weaknesses, opportunities, and challenges to determine what resources and skills you can leverage and what obstacles you may need to overcome.

The concept of a "personal SWOT analysis" offers a useful tool for this process. By identifying internal and external factors that influence your ability to reinvent yourself, you can develop a realistic understanding of your starting point. For example, someone considering a career change might assess their transferable skills, financial stability, and potential industry trends to gauge feasibility and readiness.

This stage also involves letting go of what no longer aligns with your vision. As Laozi observed in the *Tao Te Ching*, "To attain knowledge, add things every day. To attain wisdom, subtract things every day." Letting go of outdated habits, roles, or mindsets creates space for new possibilities to emerge.

Step 3: Develop a Roadmap for Change

Reinvention requires a plan—a roadmap that outlines the steps needed to transition from your current state to your desired future. This roadmap should include both short-term actions and long-term goals, providing a clear structure for progress while allowing flexibility to adapt to unforeseen challenges.

When Satya Nadella became CEO of Microsoft, he developed a comprehensive strategy to reinvent the company's culture and business model. This roadmap prioritized innovation, collaboration, and a shift toward cloud computing, enabling Microsoft to regain its competitive edge. By setting measurable objectives and fostering a culture of continuous learning, Nadella ensured that reinvention was both purposeful and sustainable.

For individuals, creating a roadmap might involve setting milestones, establishing a timeline, and identifying specific actions to take. For example, someone pursuing a new career path might set goals such as earning relevant certifications, expanding their professional network, or gaining experience through volunteer work.

Step 4: Embrace Experimentation and Iteration

Reinvention is rarely a linear process. It often involves trial and error, with successes and setbacks along the way. Embracing experimentation allows us to test ideas, learn from outcomes, and refine our approach without fear of failure.

The iterative nature of reinvention is evident in the story of Thomas Edison, whose relentless experimentation led to the invention of the lightbulb. Edison famously said, "I have not failed. I've just found 10,000 ways that won't work." This mindset of resilience and adaptability underscores the importance of viewing reinvention as a dynamic, evolving process.

In practical terms, experimentation might involve taking small, calculated risks to explore new possibilities. For instance, someone considering a career change could start by taking on freelance projects or attending workshops in their desired field, gaining experience and confidence before making a full transition.

Step 5: Build a Support System

Reinvention is not a solitary endeavor—it thrives on connection and collaboration. Surrounding yourself with a supportive community of mentors, peers, and allies can provide encouragement, guidance, and accountability throughout the process.

The role of mentorship is particularly valuable in reinvention. A mentor who has navigated similar challenges can offer insights, share lessons learned, and help you avoid common pitfalls. Additionally, seeking feedback from trusted individuals can provide fresh perspectives and help you refine your approach.

Oprah Winfrey's success as a media mogul is a testament to the power of a strong support system. Throughout her career, she cultivated relationships with mentors and collaborators who shared her vision and believed in her potential. These connections not only amplified her impact but also reinforced her resilience during moments of uncertainty.

Step 6: Celebrate Progress and Reflect on Growth

Reinvention is as much about the journey as the destination. Celebrating small victories along the way reinforces motivation and builds momentum, reminding us of the progress we have made. Reflection is equally important, allowing us to evaluate what is working, adjust our strategies, and appreciate the personal growth that reinvention fosters.

Journaling, mindfulness practices, or periodic self-assessments can help you stay connected to your purpose and track your development. This reflective practice not only enhances self-awareness but also deepens your sense of fulfillment, making reinvention a source of joy rather than stress.

The Transformative Power of Reinvention

Reinvention is not a single event but a lifelong practice—a way of continually aligning our identities, actions, and goals with the changing landscape of our lives. By following a structured framework, we can navigate this journey with confidence and purpose, transforming challenges into opportunities for growth.

The stories of Howard Schultz, Satya Nadella, and countless others remind us that reinvention is both an art and a science, requiring vision, strategy, and resilience. It is a process that invites us to embrace change, rediscover our potential, and create lives that reflect our deepest aspirations.

As we navigate the complexities of reinvention, we are reminded of the words of Ralph Waldo Emerson: "Do not go where the path may lead, go instead where there is no path and leave a trail." Reinvention is not about following a predefined script—it is about forging new paths, expanding horizons, and unlocking the boundless possibilities within us.

CHAPTER 7: THE RESILIENT MIND – CULTIVATING INNER STRENGTH IN TURBULENT TIMES

Building Emotional Fortitude

In turbulent times, emotional fortitude serves as the bedrock of resilience. It is the capacity to remain grounded and composed in the face of adversity, to process emotions constructively, and to draw strength from inner reserves when the world around us feels unstable. Cultivating emotional fortitude requires a deliberate approach—one rooted in timeless wisdom, modern psychological practices, and a commitment to personal growth. Through frameworks like stoicism, mindfulness, and cognitive-behavioral therapy (CBT), we can develop the emotional resilience needed to navigate life's challenges with grace and strength.

The Stoic Approach to Emotional Strength

Stoicism, an ancient Greek and Roman philosophy, offers profound insights into building emotional fortitude. Central to stoicism is the idea that while we cannot control external events, we can control our perceptions and reactions to them. This principle is encapsulated in the words of Epictetus, a former slave turned philosopher: "It's not what happens to you, but how you react to it that matters."

The stoic practice of distinguishing between what is within our control and what is not helps cultivate emotional resilience. By focusing on our thoughts, actions, and attitudes, we learn to let go of anxiety about things beyond our influence. For example, a person facing a job loss might channel their energy into updating their skills and seeking new opportunities rather than dwelling on the unfairness of the situation.

The stoic technique of premeditatio malorum, or "the premeditation of evils," further strengthens emotional fortitude. By imagining potential setbacks and preparing ourselves mentally for their occurrence, we become less overwhelmed when challenges arise. This practice does not promote pessimism but rather equips us to face life's uncertainties with calm determination.

Mindfulness: Anchoring the Present

While stoicism emphasizes rational control of emotions, mindfulness offers a complementary approach by fostering nonjudgmental awareness of the present moment. Rooted in ancient

Buddhist traditions and widely adopted in modern psychology, mindfulness teaches us to observe our thoughts and emotions without becoming entangled in them.

Mindfulness-based stress reduction (MBSR), a program developed by Dr. Jon Kabat-Zinn, has demonstrated remarkable effectiveness in enhancing emotional resilience. By practicing mindfulness, individuals learn to respond to stressors with clarity and intention rather than reacting impulsively. For instance, during a heated argument, a mindful person might pause to take a deep breath and reflect before responding, de-escalating the situation and preserving their emotional balance.

One key mindfulness practice is body scanning, which involves directing attention to different parts of the body to identify and release tension. This exercise not only promotes physical relaxation but also heightens awareness of how emotions manifest in the body. Over time, this awareness fosters greater emotional regulation and resilience.

Cognitive-Behavioral Techniques for Resil-

ience

Cognitive-behavioral therapy (CBT), a widely used psychological approach, provides practical tools for developing emotional fortitude. At its core, CBT is based on the idea that our thoughts, emotions, and behaviors are interconnected. By identifying and challenging negative thought patterns, we can reshape our emotional responses and adopt healthier coping mechanisms.

One CBT technique that builds resilience is cognitive restructuring. This involves examining automatic negative thoughts—such as "I'll never succeed" or "Everything is going wrong"—and replacing them with balanced, evidence-based perspectives. For example, instead of dwelling on a failed project as a sign of personal inadequacy, we might reframe it as a learning opportunity that contributes to growth.

Another valuable CBT practice is exposure therapy, which involves gradually confronting fears or discomforts in a controlled manner. This technique helps desensitize individuals to triggers, reducing their emotional intensity over time. For example, someone with social anxiety might begin by attending small gatherings before progressing to larger events, building confidence and resilience incrementally.

Historical Examples of Emotional Fortitude

The principles of stoicism, mindfulness, and CBT are not abstract theories—they have been demonstrated in the lives of individuals who exemplify emotional resilience. One such figure is Viktor Frankl, an Austrian psychiatrist and Holocaust survivor. During his imprisonment in Nazi concentration camps, Frankl endured unimaginable suffering, yet he found meaning and purpose even in the darkest circumstances.

In his seminal work, *Man's Search for Meaning*, Frankl wrote, "Everything can be taken from a man but one thing: the last of the human freedoms—to choose one's attitude in any given set of circumstances." By focusing on his inner response to external horrors, Frankl maintained his emotional strength and inspired countless others to do the same.

Frankl's story underscores the power of perspective in cultivating resilience. By aligning our thoughts and actions with our values, we can find meaning even in adversity, strengthening our emotional fortitude in the process.

Practical Applications for Everyday Life

Building emotional fortitude is not limited to extraordinary circumstances—it is a skill that can be practiced and applied in daily life. One practical approach is journaling, which provides a structured outlet for processing emotions and gaining clarity. Writing about challenges, reflections, and intentions helps organize thoughts, reduce emotional overwhelm, and foster a sense of control.

Another practice is gratitude, which shifts our focus from what is lacking to what is present. Studies in positive psychology have shown that expressing gratitude enhances emotional well-being and resilience. Keeping a gratitude journal, where we regularly list things we are thankful for, cultivates a mindset of abundance and optimism, even in difficult times.

Finally, engaging in regular physical activity, such as yoga or walking, supports emotional resilience by reducing stress hormones and promoting a sense of balance. Exercise not only benefits the body but also sharpens the mind, helping us approach challenges with greater clarity and resolve.

The Path to Emotional Fortitude

Cultivating emotional fortitude is a journey of self-awareness, practice, and growth. By drawing on the wisdom of stoicism, the mindfulness of presence, and the actionable tools of CBT, we can build the inner strength to face life's challenges with courage and grace. The examples of Viktor Frankl and others remind us that resilience is not about eliminating adversity but about rising above it, discovering our capacity to endure and thrive.

In a world of constant change and uncertainty, emotional fortitude is the anchor that keeps us steady. It is a skill that grows stronger with use, enabling us to navigate turbulence with resilience and transform obstacles into opportunities for growth. Through deliberate effort and reflection, we can cultivate the emotional strength to embrace life's complexities and emerge stronger on the other side.

The Role of Community in Resilience

Resilience is often thought of as a deeply personal quality, forged through individual strength and determination. Yet, history and psychology reveal that the support of a community is an indispensable pillar of resilience. A strong network of relationships can provide emotional encouragement, practical assistance, and a sense of belonging that empowers individuals to endure and overcome even the most trying circumstances. Whether through the collective perseverance of societies in crisis or the quiet strength found in personal support systems, community plays a vital role in cultivating resilience.

The Blitz Spirit: Collective Resilience in Adversity

One of the most striking examples of community resilience is found in the Blitz, a series of sustained bombing campaigns on Britain during World War II. Between 1940 and 1941, London and other cities faced relentless air raids, which destroyed homes, disrupted daily life, and instilled widespread fear. Yet, rather than succumbing to despair, the British people displayed remarkable fortitude—a phenomenon often referred to as the "Blitz spirit."

This collective resilience was not born from individual efforts alone but from the strength of community bonds. Neighbors supported one another in shelters, sharing resources and comforting words. Civilians volunteered for fire-fighting brigades, first aid teams, and rescue efforts, transforming ordinary citizens into everyday heroes. Social gatherings, even amid the rubble, provided moments of joy and normalcy, reinforcing the human need for connection.

The Blitz spirit exemplifies the power of shared purpose in fostering resilience. When individuals come together to face adversity, they draw strength not only from their own reserves but also from the collective energy of their community. This interconnectedness transforms fear into courage and isolation into solidarity, enabling societies to endure hardships that might otherwise seem insurmountable.

Modern Support Groups: Resilience in Every-day Life

While the Blitz spirit represents an extraordinary instance of community resilience, the same principles apply to more ordinary challenges in modern life. Support groups, whether formal or informal, provide a space for individuals to share experiences, offer advice, and find solace in the understanding of others.

Consider Alcoholics Anonymous (AA), one of the most well-known examples of a community-based approach to resilience. Founded in 1935, AA has helped millions of individuals recover from addiction by fostering a sense of accountability and connection. The program's emphasis on mutual support and shared experience creates an environment where members feel seen, heard, and empowered to change.

Similarly, online communities have emerged as vital sources of support in the digital age. Platforms such as Reddit, Facebook groups, and dedicated forums allow individuals facing common challenges—be it parenting, chronic illness, or career transitions—to connect and share resources. These virtual networks break down geographical barriers, enabling people to find community even when physical proximity is not possible.

The Science of Connection

The role of community in resilience is supported by scientific research, which highlights the profound impact of social connections on mental health and well-being. Studies in positive psychology have shown that individuals with strong social networks are more likely to cope effectively with stress, recover from trauma, and maintain a sense of purpose.

Neuroscience provides further insights into this phenomenon. When we experience social support, our brains release oxytocin, often referred to as the "bonding hormone." This chemical not only strengthens feelings of trust and connection but also reduces stress and enhances emotional regulation. In times of crisis, these physiological responses can make the difference between feeling overwhelmed and finding the strength to persevere.

Moreover, the concept of "social buffering" suggests that the presence of supportive relationships can mitigate the negative effects of stress. For example, a study on caregivers of Alzheimer's patients found that those with strong social ties reported lower levels of depression and anxiety than their isolated counterparts. This underscores the importance of fostering meaningful connections as a foundation for resilience.

Lessons from Philosophy: The Role of Community in Flourishing

The importance of community in resilience is not a new discovery—it has been a central theme in philosophical thought for centuries. Aristotle, in his writings on human flourishing, argued that humans are inherently social beings. He believed that friendships and communal bonds are essential for achieving eudaimonia, or a state of deep well-being and fulfillment.

Similarly, the African philosophy of Ubuntu emphasizes the interconnectedness of humanity. The phrase "I am because we are" captures the essence of Ubuntu, which values compassion, mutual care, and shared identity as the foundation of a thriving community. These philosophical perspectives remind us that resilience is not just about individual strength but about drawing from the collective power of our shared humanity.

Building and Nurturing Resilient Communities

Creating and maintaining resilient communities requires intentional effort. It begins with cultivating relationships based on trust, empathy, and reciprocity. Acts of kindness—whether offering a listening ear, helping a neighbor, or volunteering for a cause—strengthen the bonds that hold communities together.

One practical way to foster community resilience is through regular gatherings, such as family dinners, neighborhood events, or workplace check-ins. These interactions provide opportunities to share experiences, celebrate achievements, and support one another through challenges.

For individuals seeking to build their personal support networks, joining clubs, organizations, or online groups aligned with their interests can be a valuable starting point. Engaging in shared activities creates a sense of belonging and opens the door to meaningful connections.

The Balance of Giving and Receiving

Community resilience thrives on a balance of giving and receiving. While it is important to seek support when needed, contributing to the well-being of others can also enhance one's own resilience. Helping others fosters a sense of purpose, strengthens social bonds, and reinforces the idea that we are not alone in our struggles.

The concept of "mutual aid" captures this dynamic. Mutual aid involves communities coming together to address shared challenges, pooling resources and expertise for the collective good. This approach was evident during the COVID-19 pandemic, when grassroots organizations mobilized to deliver groceries, provide childcare, and support frontline workers. These acts of solidarity demonstrated the transformative power of community in times of crisis.

The Ripple Effect of Resilient Communities

When communities prioritize connection and support, their resilience extends beyond the individuals within them. Resilient communities inspire others, create ripple effects of positivity, and contribute to broader social stability. The lessons of the Blitz spirit, modern support groups, and mutual aid initiatives remind us that resilience is not just an individual endeavor—it is a collective journey, strengthened by the ties that bind us together.

As we navigate the challenges of an increasingly complex world, the role of community in resilience becomes ever more vital. By fostering connections, offering support, and embracing our shared humanity, we can create a foundation of strength that sustains us through even the most turbulent times.

Overcoming Mental Barriers

Resilience often hinges not on the absence of challenges but on how we address the internal obstacles that stand in our way. Mental barriers—such as fear, negativity, and self-doubt—can sap our strength and prevent us from responding effectively to adversity. Yet, these barriers are not insurmountable. By identifying their origins, reframing our thoughts, and cultivating constructive habits, we can dismantle these obstacles and unlock the inner resources needed to thrive in turbulent times.

The Paralyzing Power of Fear

Fear, at its core, is a natural response to perceived danger. It alerts us to threats and readies the body for action, but when unchecked, it can become a paralyzing force. Fear of failure, rejection, or the unknown often leads to avoidance and inaction, limiting our ability to grow and adapt.

Franklin D. Roosevelt's famous words, "The only thing we have to fear is fear itself," capture the essence of this challenge. During the Great Depression, fear of economic collapse had gripped the nation, eroding confidence and stalling recovery. Roosevelt's leadership emphasized confronting fear directly, inspiring individuals and communities to take courageous steps toward rebuilding their lives.

To overcome fear, it is essential to understand its origins and challenge its grip on our thoughts. One effective technique is gradual exposure, a principle borrowed from cognitive-behavioral therapy (CBT). By confronting fears incrementally—such as speaking up in a small group before addressing a larger audience—we build confidence and reduce fear's power over time. This approach transforms fear from a barrier into a stepping stone for growth.

Negativity: The Lens That Distorts Reality

Negativity often acts as a mental filter, skewing our perception of events and reinforcing a sense of helplessness. When negativity dominates, even minor setbacks can feel insurmountable, and opportunities for growth may go unnoticed. This phenomenon is closely tied to the concept of negativity bias, the brain's tendency to prioritize negative experiences over positive ones.

Victor Hugo's *Les Misérables* offers a poignant exploration of overcoming negativity. Jean Valjean, the novel's protagonist, begins as a man consumed by bitterness and despair after years of imprisonment. Through acts of kindness and self-reflection, he gradually shifts his perspective, finding purpose and redemption. Valjean's journey reminds us that negativity, while deeply ingrained, can be reshaped through intentional effort.

Reframing is a powerful tool for counteracting negativity. This cognitive strategy involves interpreting challenges in a way that highlights opportunities for learning and growth. For example, instead of viewing a failed job interview as a reflection of personal inadequacy, we might see it as a chance to refine our skills and approach future opportunities with greater preparedness.

The Inner Critic: Battling Self-Doubt

Self-doubt, often fueled by an overactive inner critic, undermines resilience by casting doubt on our abilities and worth. This mental barrier can manifest as perfectionism, fear of judgment, or an incessant comparison to others. Left unchecked, self-doubt can erode confidence and prevent us from pursuing meaningful goals.

To quiet the inner critic, it is essential to cultivate self-compassion. Dr. Kristin Neff, a leading researcher in this field, emphasizes the importance of treating ourselves with the same kindness and understanding that we would offer a close friend. Self-compassion involves acknowledging our imperfections without judgment and recognizing that setbacks are a natural part of the human experience.

Consider the example of J.K. Rowling, whose journey to success was fraught with rejection and self-doubt. Before the *Harry Potter* series became a global phenomenon, Rowling faced numerous rejections from publishers. Instead of allowing self-doubt to derail her aspirations, she drew on inner resilience and the support of her community to persevere. Her story highlights the transformative power of self-compassion and determination in overcoming mental barriers.

The Role of Thought Patterns in Resilience

Our thought patterns play a significant role in shaping our resilience. Automatic negative thoughts, or ANTs, often arise unconsciously and reinforce feelings of helplessness. These thoughts may include overgeneralizations ("I always fail"), catastrophizing ("This will ruin everything"), or personalizing ("This is all my fault").

One effective method for addressing ANTs is cognitive restructuring, a technique rooted in CBT. This process involves identifying negative thought patterns, evaluating their validity, and replacing them with balanced perspectives. For instance, when faced with a setback, we might challenge the thought, "I'm a failure," by recalling past successes and recognizing the specific factors that contributed to the current challenge.

Mindfulness practices also play a crucial role in breaking the cycle of negative thought patterns. By observing our thoughts without judgment, we create space to choose more constructive responses. This awareness allows us to detach from unhelpful narratives and approach challenges with greater clarity and resilience.

Breaking the Cycle of Mental Barriers

Overcoming mental barriers requires consistent effort and intentionality. Developing new habits, such as journaling, gratitude exercises, or seeking feedback from trusted peers, can reinforce positive thought patterns and build emotional strength.

Journaling, for example, provides a structured outlet for processing emotions and gaining insight into recurring thought patterns. By reflecting on challenges and identifying lessons learned, we shift our focus from obstacles to opportunities for growth.

Gratitude exercises, such as listing three things we are thankful for each day, counteract negativity bias by redirecting attention to the positive aspects of our lives. Over time, this practice fosters a more optimistic and resilient mindset.

Seeking feedback from trusted individuals offers a valuable external perspective, helping us identify blind spots and reframe challenges in constructive ways. Engaging in open, honest dialogue with mentors or peers can provide the encouragement and insight needed to navigate mental barriers effectively.

The Transformative Power of Reframing

Reframing is not just a cognitive exercise—it is a mindset that transforms how we engage with the world. By shifting our perspective, we reclaim agency over our thoughts and actions, breaking free from the constraints of fear, negativity, and self-doubt.

Consider the example of Helen Keller, who overcame the profound barriers of blindness and deafness to become a renowned author, activist, and speaker. Keller's ability to reframe her limitations as opportunities for growth and contribution exemplifies the resilience that emerges from overcoming mental barriers. Her story serves as a powerful reminder that our greatest obstacles often hold the seeds of our greatest strengths.

The Path Forward

Overcoming mental barriers is not a one-time effort but an ongoing process of self-awareness, reflection, and growth. By addressing fear, negativity, and self-doubt with intentional strategies, we build the foundation for a resilient mind. The tools of reframing, mindfulness, and self-compassion empower us to navigate life's challenges with courage and clarity, transforming internal obstacles into stepping stones for personal and professional fulfillment.

Resilience is not the absence of adversity—it is the ability to rise above it. As we confront and overcome our mental barriers, we unlock the full potential of our inner strength, enabling us to thrive in an ever-changing world.

Daily Practices for Resilience

Resilience, like any skill, is cultivated through consistent practice. While moments of crisis may test our inner strength, it is the daily habits we nurture that prepare us to meet these challenges with clarity, courage, and composure. By incorporating intentional practices into our routines, we create a foundation of resilience that grows stronger over time. These practices—rooted in reflection, mindfulness, and gratitude—not only enhance our ability to cope with adversity but also foster a deeper sense of fulfillment and connection in everyday life.

Journaling: A Mirror for the Mind

Journaling is one of the most powerful tools for building resilience, offering a structured outlet for self-reflection and emotional processing. By putting thoughts to paper, we gain clarity about our experiences, identify patterns in our thinking, and uncover insights that might otherwise remain hidden.

The American author and naturalist Henry David Thoreau famously kept detailed journals during his time at Walden Pond, where he sought to live deliberately and reflect on life's essentials. His writings reveal not only his philosophical musings but also his ability to navigate solitude and uncertainty with grace. For Thoreau, journaling was a means of connecting with his inner self and cultivating a resilient mindset.

In practice, journaling can take many forms. Some individuals use it to process difficult emotions, while others focus on setting intentions, celebrating achievements, or exploring creative ideas. A simple technique is the "three-question approach," where each entry addresses three prompts: What happened today? How did it make me feel? What can I learn from it? This method encourages both self-awareness and growth, turning everyday experiences into opportunities for resilience.

Meditation: Anchoring the Present

Meditation, a practice that has been cultivated for centuries, offers profound benefits for resilience by training the mind to remain present and composed amid life's turbulence. At its core, meditation involves focusing attention—whether on the breath, a mantra, or bodily sensations—and gently redirecting it whenever distractions arise.

Scientific research supports the transformative effects of meditation on resilience. Studies in neuroscience have shown that mindfulness meditation can reduce activity in the amygdala, the brain's fear center, while strengthening connections in the prefrontal cortex, which governs rational decision-making. These changes enhance our ability to respond to stressors with calmness and clarity.

Consider the example of Jon Kabat-Zinn, the

founder of Mindfulness-Based Stress Reduction (MBSR). Kabat-Zinn developed this program to help individuals manage chronic pain and stress through mindfulness meditation. Over time, MBSR has been widely adopted in clinical and corporate settings, demonstrating its effectiveness in building resilience across diverse contexts.

For those new to meditation, starting with just five to ten minutes a day can yield meaningful benefits. Apps like Headspace or Calm provide guided sessions that make the practice accessible and adaptable to modern lifestyles. Over time, meditation becomes a sanctuary — a space to recharge, reflect, and reconnect with one's inner strength.

Gratitude: Shifting the Perspective

Gratitude is a practice that transforms the way we perceive the world, shifting focus from what is lacking to what is abundant. By cultivating a mindset of gratitude, we build resilience through the recognition of life's blessings, even in the face of challenges.

During the American Civil War, President Abraham Lincoln often turned to gratitude as a source of strength. In 1863, amid the war's hardships, Lincoln issued the Thanksgiving Proclamation, urging Americans to reflect on the nation's enduring blessings. This act of fostering gratitude not only united a divided country but also demonstrated the power of gratitude to inspire resilience in the darkest times.

A practical way to incorporate gratitude into daily life is through a gratitude journal. Each day, take a moment to write down three things you are thankful for. These can be as simple as a kind gesture from a stranger or as profound as the support of a loved one. Over time, this practice rewires the brain to focus on positivity, creating a buffer against negativity and stress.

Physical Activity: Resilience in Motion

Resilience is not solely a mental or emotional endeavor—it is also deeply tied to physical well-being. Engaging in regular physical activity, whether through exercise, yoga, or even a brisk walk, strengthens the body and enhances the mind's capacity to cope with adversity.

The physiological effects of exercise on resilience are well-documented. Physical activity reduces stress hormones such as cortisol while increasing endorphins, the body's natural mood elevators. These biochemical changes not only improve mood but also enhance cognitive function, enabling us to approach challenges with greater focus and determination.

Yoga, in particular, offers a holistic approach to resilience by integrating movement, breathwork, and mindfulness. The ancient practice of yoga emphasizes balance and flexibility, both physically and mentally. Asanas, or poses, teach us to find stability in discomfort, mirroring the resilience required in life's challenges.

Connection: A Daily Anchor

While resilience often begins within, it is nourished through connection with others. Making time each day to engage with loved ones, share experiences, or simply express appreciation strengthens the bonds that sustain us. These moments of connection remind us that we are not alone in our struggles, fostering a sense of belonging and mutual support.

One way to deepen connections is through active listening. When engaging with others, focus fully on their words, emotions, and intentions, setting aside distractions and judgments. This practice not only strengthens relationships but also cultivates empathy and understanding—qualities that enhance resilience in both personal and communal contexts.

Integration and Reflection

Daily practices for resilience are most effective when integrated into a routine that reflects your values and goals. Whether through morning meditation, an evening gratitude journal, or a midday walk, these practices create anchors that ground us in stability and purpose. Over time, they become second nature, infusing resilience into every aspect of life.

Reflection is a key component of this integration. At the end of each week, take a moment to review your practices and their impact. What felt meaningful? What could be improved? This process of reflection not only reinforces consistency but also deepens your understanding of resilience as a dynamic, evolving skill.

The Cumulative Power of Daily Practices

Resilience is not built in a single moment—it is the result of countless small actions taken consistently over time. Journaling, meditation, gratitude, physical activity, and connection are not merely habits; they are investments in your inner strength and well-being. Each practice, like a brick in a foundation, contributes to the stability and resilience needed to navigate life's uncertainties.

As we weave these practices into our daily lives, we discover the transformative power of intentionality. Resilience becomes not just a response to adversity but a way of being—a mindset that empowers us to embrace challenges, celebrate joys, and find meaning in the journey. In the words of the poet Rainer Maria Rilke, "The only journey is the one within." Through daily practices, we embark on this journey, cultivating the resilience that allows us to flourish, no matter what lies ahead.

CHAPTER 8:
THE FUTURE OF
REINVENTION –
INNOVATING IN AN
EVER-CHANGING
WORLD

Navigating Modern Challenges

The world today is evolving at an unprecedented pace, driven by technological advancements, global interconnectivity, and societal transformations. In this dynamic environment, the ability to adapt and reinvent oneself is no longer a luxury—it is a necessity. To navigate modern challenges, individuals and organizations must embrace a mindset of curiosity, flexibility, and proactive innovation. By understanding the forces shaping our world and drawing insights from futurists and global trends, we can chart a path toward resilience and reinvention in an ever-changing landscape.

The Acceleration of Change

Technological progress has always been a catalyst for societal transformation, but the speed at which innovations are emerging today is unparalleled. The Fourth Industrial Revolution—a term coined by Klaus Schwab, founder of the World Economic Forum—describes the convergence of technologies such as artificial intelligence, robotics, blockchain, and biotechnology. These advancements are not only reshaping industries but also redefining how we work, communicate, and live.

For instance, the rise of automation and artificial intelligence has transformed traditional labor markets, creating both opportunities and challenges. While some jobs are being rendered obsolete, new roles are emerging in fields such as data science, renewable energy, and digital marketing. To remain relevant, workers must continuously update their skills, often transitioning into entirely new career paths. This trend underscores the importance of lifelong learning as a cornerstone of resilience in the modern age.

Beyond technology, societal shifts are influencing the need for reinvention. The growing emphasis on sustainability, diversity, and social responsibility is prompting businesses to re-evaluate their values and practices. Companies that fail to adapt to these cultural imperatives risk losing relevance in a world where consumers increasingly demand ethical and inclusive solutions.

Insights from Futurists

Futurists, experts who study patterns and trends to anticipate the possibilities of tomorrow, provide valuable insights into navigating modern challenges. Alvin Toffler, a pioneering futurist, famously predicted in his book *Future Shock* that the rate of change would outpace humanity's ability to cope, leading to widespread disorientation. His work emphasized the importance of adaptability and foresight in managing the pressures of an accelerated future.

One of Toffler's key ideas was the concept of "learn, unlearn, and relearn." This principle highlights the need to let go of outdated knowledge and acquire new skills to stay relevant in a rapidly evolving world. It serves as a reminder that reinvention is not a one-time event but an ongoing process of growth and renewal.

Another influential futurist, Ray Kurzweil, advocates for embracing technological change as a means of enhancing human potential. Kurzweil's theory of the "singularity"—a future point where artificial intelligence surpasses human intelligence—illustrates both the challenges and opportunities of technological advancement. While some fear the implications of AI, Kurzweil emphasizes the potential for collaboration between humans and machines to solve complex global problems.

These futurists underscore the importance of viewing change not as a threat but as an opportunity for innovation. By adopting a proactive mindset and staying attuned to emerging trends, we can position ourselves to thrive in an uncertain future.

Global Trends Shaping Reinvention

Several global trends are shaping the need for reinvention, highlighting the interconnected nature of modern challenges. Climate change, for example, is driving innovation across industries as societies grapple with the urgency of sustainability. From renewable energy solutions to circular economies, the push for environmental responsibility is transforming how we produce, consume, and interact with the planet.

The COVID-19 pandemic further underscored the necessity of adaptability. As businesses and individuals faced unprecedented disruptions, many turned to technology to maintain continuity. Remote work, telemedicine, and online education became the norm, demonstrating the power of digital transformation to enable resilience. At the same time, the pandemic revealed the importance of mental health and social connection, prompting a reevaluation of priorities and values.

Globalization, while fostering collaboration and innovation, also presents unique challenges. The interconnectedness of economies and cultures means that local events can have far-reaching impacts, as seen in supply chain disruptions and geopolitical tensions. Navigating these complexities requires a deep understanding of global dynamics and the ability to adapt to diverse contexts.

The Human Element in Reinvention

Amid the technological and societal changes shaping our world, the human element remains at the heart of reinvention. Emotional intelligence, creativity, and ethical decision-making are increasingly valued in a landscape where machines can perform routine tasks. These uniquely human qualities enable us to navigate ambiguity, build meaningful relationships, and envision possibilities beyond the status quo.

Philosopher Yuval Noah Harari, in his book *21 Lessons for the 21st Century*, explores the intersection of technology and humanity, emphasizing the need for self-awareness and adaptability. Harari argues that in a world of constant change, the ability to reinvent oneself is a key determinant of success and fulfillment. His call for introspection and resilience resonates with the challenges and opportunities of our time.

Practical Strategies for Navigating Modern Challenges

To navigate modern challenges, individuals and organizations must cultivate a mindset of continuous learning and proactive adaptation. This begins with staying informed about emerging trends and seeking out diverse perspectives. Engaging with thought leaders, attending industry conferences, and participating in online communities can provide valuable insights into the forces shaping our world.

Another critical strategy is embracing experimentation and iteration. Just as startups use
agile methodologies to test and refine ideas,
individuals can adopt a similar approach to
personal and professional growth. Whether
exploring new hobbies, pursuing additional
education, or taking on stretch assignments
at work, small steps toward reinvention build
the confidence and skills needed to thrive in a
changing environment.

Finally, fostering resilience requires a commitment to well-being. In the face of constant
demands and distractions, practices such as
mindfulness, exercise, and meaningful social
connections provide the foundation for sustained adaptability. By prioritizing self-care,
we equip ourselves to meet the challenges of
modern life with clarity and strength.

The Promise of Reinvention

Navigating modern challenges demands more
than mere survival—it calls for a spirit of innovation, curiosity, and resilience. By understanding the forces shaping our world and embracing
the tools of reinvention, we can not only adapt

to change but also shape the future with intention and purpose. As we navigate the complexities of the 21st century, the ability to reinvent ourselves remains our greatest asset, enabling us to rise to the challenges of today and seize the opportunities of tomorrow.

Lessons from Innovators

Reinvention is a hallmark of visionary leaders who shape the future. These innovators challenge conventions, embrace uncertainty, and continually evolve to address emerging opportunities and challenges. By examining the stories of modern visionaries like Elon Musk, Jeff Bezos, and others, we gain valuable insights into the principles and practices that drive transformative reinvention. Their journeys illuminate not only the power of adaptability but also the courage and creativity required to redefine industries and inspire change.

Elon Musk: Reinventing the Possible

Elon Musk epitomizes the spirit of relentless reinvention. From electric vehicles and space exploration to renewable energy and artificial intelligence, Musk's ventures have redefined entire industries. His ability to envision and execute audacious ideas stems from a mindset that sees challenges not as barriers but as opportunities to innovate.

Tesla, perhaps Musk's most iconic enterprise, began as a bold bet in an industry dominated by internal combustion engines. When traditional automakers dismissed the viability of electric vehicles, Musk doubled down, investing personal resources and championing a vision of sustainable transportation. Despite early skepticism and financial struggles, Tesla transformed the automotive landscape, proving that reinvention often requires persistence in the face of doubt.

SpaceX, another of Musk's ventures, exemplifies his approach to tackling seemingly insurmountable challenges. At a time when space exploration was largely the domain of government agencies, Musk set out to make space travel more affordable and accessible. SpaceX's breakthroughs, such as reusable rockets, reflect not only technological ingenuity but also a willingness to question established norms. Musk's journey underscores the importance of taking calculated risks and maintaining a long-term vision, even when immediate results seem elusive.

Jeff Bezos: Building the Everything Store

Jeff Bezos, the founder of Amazon, offers another compelling example of reinvention. What began as an online bookstore has evolved into a global technology giant, revolutionizing retail, logistics, cloud computing, and entertainment. Bezos's ability to anticipate trends and adapt Amazon's strategy highlights the importance of agility and customer-centric innovation.

Bezos's leadership philosophy, encapsulated in the principle of "Day 1," emphasizes the importance of maintaining a startup mentality regardless of an organization's size. By fostering a culture of experimentation and continuous improvement, Amazon has remained at the forefront of innovation. Initiatives like Amazon Prime, AWS (Amazon Web Services), and Alexa demonstrate the power of reinvention to expand possibilities and redefine consumer experiences.

A key lesson from Bezos's journey is the value

of thinking big while starting small. Each of Amazon's groundbreaking ventures began with a focus on solving specific customer problems, such as faster delivery or affordable cloud storage. Over time, these incremental innovations built the foundation for transformational change.

Indra Nooyi: Reinventing Leadership

Indra Nooyi, former CEO of PepsiCo, provides a different yet equally inspiring perspective on reinvention. Under her leadership, Pepsi-Co shifted its focus toward sustainability and health-conscious products, reflecting changing consumer preferences and societal demands. Nooyi's emphasis on "performance with purpose" redefined the company's mission, integrating profitability with social responsibility.

Nooyi's approach to reinvention highlights the importance of aligning business strategy with evolving values. By championing initiatives such as reducing sugar content and promoting environmental stewardship, she positioned PepsiCo as a leader in corporate responsibility. Her journey demonstrates that reinvention is not solely about adapting to external trends but also about driving meaningful change from within.

Reid Hoffman: Scaling the Vision

Reid Hoffman, co-founder of LinkedIn, offers insights into the role of networks and collaboration in reinvention. LinkedIn's success as a professional networking platform reflects Hoffman's ability to identify untapped opportunities and scale ideas effectively. His philosophy, outlined in his book *Blitzscaling*, emphasizes the importance of speed and adaptability in high-growth environments.

Hoffman's approach to reinvention involves leveraging networks to amplify impact. By connecting professionals worldwide, LinkedIn has not only transformed job searching and recruiting but also fostered a culture of knowledge sharing and career development. Hoffman's journey underscores the power of community and strategic partnerships in driving innovation.

Common Threads in Reinvention

The stories of Musk, Bezos, Nooyi, Hoffman,

and others reveal common principles that underpin successful reinvention:

1. **Visionary Thinking**: Innovators imagine possibilities beyond current constraints, challenging the status quo and redefining what is possible.

2. **Calculated Risk-Taking**: Reinvention often involves stepping into the unknown. Successful leaders embrace uncertainty, balancing boldness with informed decision-making.

3. **Continuous Learning**: Staying ahead in a rapidly changing world requires a commitment to learning and adapting. Innovators remain curious and open to new ideas, constantly refining their strategies.

4. **Customer Focus**: Whether addressing individual needs or societal demands, reinvention thrives on understanding and serving the target audience.

5. **Resilience in Adversity**: Reinvention is rarely a linear path. Setbacks and challenges are inevitable, but perseverance and adaptability pave

the way to success.

Practical Applications for Reinvention

The lessons from these visionaries extend beyond the realm of industry leaders—they are equally applicable to individuals seeking personal or professional growth. For instance, embracing a mindset of continuous improvement can help anyone stay relevant in a competitive job market. Similarly, cultivating resilience and adaptability allows individuals to navigate career transitions, entrepreneurial ventures, or other life changes with confidence.

Consider how Musk's emphasis on long-term vision can inspire someone pursuing a challenging goal. By breaking the goal into smaller, actionable steps and maintaining focus on the broader purpose, individuals can overcome obstacles and achieve meaningful progress. Likewise, Bezos's principle of "Day 1" encourages individuals to approach each day with curiosity, energy, and a willingness to innovate.

The Ripple Effect of Reinvention

The impact of reinvention extends far beyond the individuals and organizations driving it. Each act of innovation creates a ripple effect, inspiring others to think differently and pursue their own transformations. Whether through technological breakthroughs, cultural shifts, or personal growth, reinvention shapes the world in profound and lasting ways.

As we draw lessons from the lives and work of modern visionaries, we are reminded that reinvention is not a privilege reserved for the extraordinary—it is a possibility open to all. By adopting the principles of curiosity, courage, and continuous learning, we too can become agents of change, contributing to a future defined by creativity, purpose, and possibility.

Reinvention as a Lifelong Practice

Reinvention is not a singular event but an ongoing process of growth, adaptation, and discovery. As the world evolves, so too must we, reshaping our identities and skills to align with shifting circumstances and aspirations. Embracing reinvention as a lifelong practice requires a mindset of curiosity, resilience, and openness to change. Through the stories of individuals who have reinvented themselves multiple times, we gain inspiration and insights into navigating the complexities of continuous growth.

The Evolution of Identity

At the heart of lifelong reinvention is the recognition that identity is not fixed but fluid. Each phase of life presents new challenges and opportunities, inviting us to explore uncharted paths. For some, this means pivoting careers or learning new skills; for others, it involves rediscovering passions or redefining relationships. The ability to embrace these transitions with courage and intentionality is what distinguishes those who thrive in an ever-changing world.

Consider the journey of Maya Angelou, the celebrated author, poet, and activist. Angelou's life was marked by a series of profound reinventions. She began as a dancer and singer, performing in nightclubs and touring internationally. Later, she became a journalist in Africa, writing for publications in Ghana and Egypt. Eventually, Angelou emerged as a literary icon with her groundbreaking memoir *I Know Why the Caged*

Bird Sings.

Angelou's multifaceted career demonstrates the power of adaptability and the importance of following one's evolving interests. Her willingness to step into unfamiliar roles and embrace new opportunities not only enriched her own life but also left a lasting legacy of creativity and empowerment.

The Mindset of Continuous Learning

A key component of lifelong reinvention is a commitment to continuous learning. This mindset involves seeking out new knowledge, skills, and experiences that expand our horizons and prepare us for future challenges. It also requires humility—the willingness to acknowledge gaps in our understanding and the courage to pursue growth, even in areas where we feel uncertain.

Former U.S. President Theodore Roosevelt embodied this spirit of continuous learning. Known for his insatiable curiosity, Roosevelt was a prolific reader, naturalist, and adventurer who pursued a wide range of interests throughout his life. After leaving the presidency, he embarked on an expedition to South America, mapping uncharted territories and immersing himself in scientific exploration. His ability to adapt to new roles and challenges underscores the importance of lifelong curiosity and intellectual engagement.

In the modern era, the pace of change demands that we adopt a similar mindset. Technologies such as artificial intelligence, blockchain, and quantum computing are reshaping industries at an unprecedented rate, creating both opportunities and disruptions. To remain relevant, individuals must continuously update their skills and stay informed about emerging trends. Online learning platforms, industry certifications, and professional networks offer accessible pathways for acquiring new expertise, empowering us to navigate an ever-changing landscape.

Resilience Through Reinvention

Lifelong reinvention is not without its challenges. Transitions often involve moments of uncertainty, self-doubt, and even failure. Yet, it is through these experiences that we build resilience and discover our capacity for growth.

The stories of individuals who have reinvented themselves multiple times reveal that setbacks are not endpoints but stepping stones to new opportunities.

Take the example of Steve Jobs, the co-founder of Apple. In 1985, Jobs was ousted from the company he had helped build, a devastating setback that forced him to reevaluate his path. Instead of succumbing to defeat, Jobs founded NeXT, a computer company focused on cutting-edge technology, and acquired Pixar, a fledgling animation studio. Both ventures played pivotal roles in his eventual return to Apple, where he spearheaded a series of transformative innovations.

Jobs's journey illustrates the power of resilience in reinvention. By viewing challenges as opportunities for growth, he not only rebuilt his career but also revolutionized multiple industries. His story reminds us that setbacks are not the end of the road—they are an invitation to explore new directions and redefine success.

The Role of Reflection in Reinvention

While reinvention often involves action and exploration, it also requires moments of reflection. Taking the time to assess our values, strengths, and aspirations allows us to chart a course that aligns with our authentic selves. Reflection helps us identify what truly matters, guiding us toward meaningful pursuits and away from distractions that do not serve our growth.

One practical approach to fostering reflection is the practice of journaling. By writing about our experiences, goals, and challenges, we gain clarity about where we are and where we want to go. This process not only deepens self-awareness but also fosters a sense of agency, empowering us to take intentional steps toward reinvention.

Another valuable tool is seeking feedback from trusted mentors, friends, or colleagues. Honest conversations about our strengths and areas for improvement provide fresh perspectives and help us uncover opportunities for growth. By engaging in open dialogue, we expand our understanding of ourselves and the possibilities available to us.

Stories of Multiple Reinventions

The stories of individuals who have reinvented themselves multiple times offer powerful lessons in resilience and adaptability. Consider Oprah Winfrey, whose career has spanned journalism, television, philanthropy, and entrepreneurship. Each chapter of Winfrey's journey reflects her ability to pivot and evolve in response to changing circumstances and opportunities. Her commitment to self-improvement and her willingness to embrace new challenges have made her one of the most influential figures of our time.

Similarly, Michelle Obama's trajectory from corporate lawyer to First Lady and bestselling author illustrates the power of reinvention as a means of aligning personal values with professional contributions. Through initiatives like Let's Move! and Becoming, Obama has used her platform to inspire and empower others, demonstrating that reinvention is a tool not only for personal growth but also for creating positive impact.

The Legacy of Lifelong Reinvention

As we navigate the complexities of an ever-changing world, the ability to reinvent ourselves becomes a vital skill. Lifelong reinvention is not about abandoning our past but about building on it, integrating our experiences into a dynamic and evolving identity. It is a journey of discovery, resilience, and growth that empowers us to meet challenges with confidence and embrace opportunities with curiosity.

By adopting a mindset of continuous learning, reflecting on our values, and drawing inspiration from those who have reinvented themselves, we can cultivate a life of purpose and adaptability. Reinvention is not merely a response to change—it is a celebration of our capacity to grow, evolve, and thrive in a world of infinite possibilities.

Thriving in Uncertainty

Uncertainty is an inevitable aspect of life, magnified in an era defined by rapid technological advancements, global interconnectedness, and shifting societal norms. While uncertainty can provoke anxiety, it is also a catalyst for growth, innovation, and reinvention. Thriving in uncertainty requires a mindset that embraces change, strategies to navigate the unknown, and the ability to see possibilities where others see obstacles. With the right tools and perspective, uncertainty becomes not a source of fear but a gateway to new opportunities.

Reframing Uncertainty as Opportunity

The first step in thriving amid uncertainty is shifting our perspective. Instead of viewing uncertainty as a threat to stability, we can see it as a space for creativity and growth. This shift in mindset echoes the principles of stoicism, which teach us to focus on what we can control while accepting the unpredictability of external events.

Consider the example of Thomas Edison. When his laboratory burned down in 1914, destroying years of work, Edison reportedly remarked, "Thank goodness all our mistakes were burned up. Now we can start fresh." Rather than succumbing to despair, Edison saw the fire as an opportunity to rebuild and innovate. His ability to reframe a devastating setback highlights the power of perspective in navigating uncertainty.

Adopting a similar mindset involves cultivating curiosity and a willingness to explore the unknown. Uncertainty often brings with it the potential for discovery—whether of new solutions, untapped strengths, or unexpected connections. By approaching challenges with an open mind, we position ourselves to uncover opportunities that might otherwise remain hidden.

The Role of Emotional Resilience

Thriving in uncertainty also requires emotional resilience—the ability to adapt to change, recover from setbacks, and maintain a sense of purpose amid ambiguity. Emotional resilience is not an innate trait but a skill that can be developed through intentional practices such as mindfulness, self-compassion, and gratitude.

Mindfulness, for example, helps us stay grounded in the present moment, reducing the tendency to ruminate on worst-case scenarios. By focusing on what is happening now rather than what might happen in the future, we create space for thoughtful decision-making and meaningful action.

Self-compassion, as described by psychologist Kristin Neff, involves treating ourselves with kindness and understanding, especially during times of uncertainty. Acknowledging our fears and doubts without judgment allows us to navigate challenges with greater clarity and confidence.

Gratitude, too, plays a vital role in building resilience. By recognizing the positive aspects of our lives, even in uncertain times, we reinforce a sense of stability and hope. Gratitude shifts our focus from what we lack to what we have, creating a foundation for resilience and growth.

Flexibility and Adaptability in Action

Flexibility and adaptability are essential qualities for thriving in a world where change is constant. These traits enable us to pivot when plans go awry, experiment with new approaches, and embrace innovation. They also involve letting go of rigid expectations and being open to alternative paths.

The COVID-19 pandemic provides a vivid

example of adaptability in action. Businesses, schools, and individuals were forced to rethink established routines, embracing remote work, virtual learning, and telemedicine almost overnight. While these changes presented challenges, they also spurred innovation, from creative solutions for connecting with loved ones to new technologies that enhanced productivity.

For individuals, cultivating adaptability begins with a willingness to step outside of comfort zones. This might involve learning new skills, exploring unfamiliar industries, or reevaluating long-held beliefs. By embracing change as an opportunity for growth, we strengthen our ability to thrive in an unpredictable world.

Building a Support System

Uncertainty is easier to navigate when we have the support of others. Whether through personal relationships, professional networks, or community connections, a strong support system provides emotional encouragement, practical assistance, and a sense of belonging.

During World War II, the concept of the "Blitz

spirit" exemplified the power of community in fostering resilience. Londoners came together during nightly air raids, supporting one another in shelters and rebuilding their city in the aftermath of destruction. This collective strength enabled individuals to face uncertainty with courage and determination.

In modern times, support systems can take many forms, from close-knit families to online communities. Actively nurturing these connections—by reaching out to friends, joining interest groups, or participating in mentorship programs—creates a network of resources that sustains us during periods of change.

Strategic Planning Amid Uncertainty

While uncertainty often requires flexibility, it also benefits from strategic planning. Setting clear goals and identifying actionable steps provides a sense of direction, even when the path ahead is unclear. Strategic planning involves balancing long-term vision with short-term adaptability, allowing us to adjust our approach as circumstances evolve.

A practical tool for navigating uncertainty is scenario planning, a technique used by organizations to anticipate and prepare for multiple possible futures. By considering a range of outcomes and developing contingency plans, we build confidence in our ability to respond effectively to unforeseen events.

For individuals, scenario planning might involve identifying alternative career paths, creating financial safety nets, or exploring diverse skill sets. These preparations reduce anxiety and empower us to approach the unknown with a sense of agency and readiness.

The Importance of Lifelong Learning

In a world of rapid change, lifelong learning is a cornerstone of thriving in uncertainty. Staying curious and engaged enables us to adapt to new technologies, industries, and cultural shifts. Lifelong learning is not limited to formal education—it encompasses personal exploration, hands-on experiences, and the exchange of ideas with others.

Bill Gates, the co-founder of Microsoft, exemplifies the power of lifelong learning. Known for his insatiable curiosity, Gates dedicates time to reading books, attending lectures, and engaging with experts across diverse fields. His commitment to continuous learning not only fuels his innovation but also equips him to navigate the complexities of an ever-changing world.

Embracing Uncertainty as a Path to Growth

Ultimately, thriving in uncertainty requires a shift from resistance to embrace. Uncertainty is not something to be feared or avoided—it is a natural part of growth and progress. By cultivating resilience, adaptability, and a willingness to learn, we transform uncertainty into a source of strength and possibility.

In the words of poet Rainer Maria Rilke, "Live the questions now. Perhaps you will then gradually, without noticing it, live along some distant day into the answer." Thriving in uncertainty is about living the questions, exploring new horizons, and trusting in our capacity to adapt and evolve. With the right mindset and practices, we can navigate the unknown with confidence, discovering opportunities and insights that enrich our lives and shape a better future.

CONCLUSION: THE ART OF REINVENTION – A JOURNEY OF GROWTH AND POSSIBILITY

Reinvention is both an art and a journey. It is the process of continually evolving, of letting go of what no longer serves us, and embracing the opportunities presented by change. Throughout this book, we have explored the profound ways in which adaptability, resilience, and creativity empower us to navigate life's uncertainties and shape a future aligned with our deepest values.

From the wisdom of history's greatest thinkers to the stories of modern innovators, the lessons of reinvention are clear: the ability to adapt is not merely a survival mechanism but a path to flourishing in a world defined by transformation. In this concluding chapter, we reflect on the themes and insights woven throughout this journey, and we look forward to the possibilities that await those who embrace the power of reinvention.

The Power of Perspective

The foundation of reinvention lies in the power of perspective. By reframing challenges as opportunities for growth, we unlock the ability to navigate even the most turbulent times with clarity and purpose. Whether drawing from the stoicism of Marcus Aurelius or the enduring optimism of Winston Churchill, we are reminded that our mindset shapes our reality.

When we shift our focus from obstacles to possibilities, the path forward becomes clearer. This shift is not about denying hardship but about choosing to see beyond it, to the lessons and opportunities that lie on the other side. In embracing this perspective, we find the courage to move forward, even when the road is uncertain.

Letting Go to Move Forward

Reinvention requires us to release the weight of outdated beliefs, habits, and systems that no longer serve us. As we explored in the stories of societal transitions, such as the Renaissance, and personal transformations, like those of entrepreneurs leaving conventional careers to follow their passions, letting go is an act of liberation.

Letting go is not about forgetting the past but about honoring it as a stepping stone to something greater. It is an invitation to clear space for new ideas, relationships, and opportunities. As we embrace the art of release, we open ourselves to the boundless possibilities that come with a fresh start.

Taking Action with Purpose

Change does not happen in a vacuum — it requires deliberate action. The stories of the Wright brothers and Edison's persistence remind us that progress is the result of courage, experimentation, and an unwavering commitment to a vision. Action transforms ideas into reality, propelling us forward even when the path is unclear.

Reinvention is not about waiting for the perfect moment but about creating momentum through small, purposeful steps. Each action, no matter how small, builds confidence and clarity, bringing us closer to our goals. In taking action, we not only shape our own futures but inspire others to do the same.

Embracing Failure as a Teacher

Failure is an inevitable part of the journey of reinvention. Yet, as Edison's countless "failed" lightbulbs and Abraham Lincoln's political setbacks demonstrate, failure is not the end—it is a beginning. Each misstep provides valuable insights, guiding us toward a better path.

By reframing failure as a teacher, we cultivate resilience and a willingness to try again. This mindset enables us to approach challenges with curiosity and determination, knowing that each attempt brings us closer to success. In embracing failure, we transform setbacks into stepping stones, building the strength and wisdom needed to thrive.

Adaptability as Strength

In a world of constant change, adaptability is one of the greatest strengths we can cultivate. Darwin's theory of evolution teaches us that it is not the strongest or the smartest who survive, but those who are most adaptable to change. This principle applies not only to species but to individuals, organizations, and societies.

The stories of adaptable leaders, such as Theodore Roosevelt and Indra Nooyi, remind us that flexibility and openness are key to navigating uncertainty. By staying attuned to the changing landscape and remaining willing to pivot, we position ourselves to thrive in any environment.

Reinvention as a Lifelong Practice

Reinvention is not a one-time event—it is a lifelong practice. Each phase of life presents new opportunities for growth, inviting us to learn, adapt, and evolve. The journeys of Maya Angelou, Oprah Winfrey, and Steve Jobs illustrate the transformative power of embracing change throughout life.

Lifelong reinvention requires a commitment to continuous learning and self-discovery. By staying curious, seeking out new experiences, and reflecting on our values, we create a dynamic and fulfilling life. This journey is not without its challenges, but it is one of profound growth and possibility.

The Future of Reinvention

As we look to the future, the importance of re-invention becomes even more apparent. In a rapidly changing world, the ability to innovate, adapt, and thrive amid uncertainty is a critical skill. The stories of visionaries like Elon Musk and Jeff Bezos remind us that reinvention is not only about responding to change but about creating it.

The future demands that we embrace uncertainty as an opportunity for growth. By cultivating resilience, adaptability, and a willingness to explore the unknown, we position ourselves to navigate the complexities of the modern world with confidence and purpose.

A Call to Action

The journey of reinvention is deeply personal, yet its impact extends far beyond the individual. Each act of growth and transformation creates a ripple effect, inspiring those around us and contributing to a world of greater creativity, resilience, and possibility.

As you close this book, consider how the lessons of reinvention can be applied in your own life. What habits, beliefs, or practices no longer serve you? What new opportunities are waiting to be explored? How can you embrace change as a source of strength and growth?

The path of reinvention is not always easy, but it is profoundly rewarding. It invites us to step into our potential, to create a life of meaning and fulfillment, and to contribute to a brighter future for all.

In the words of Rainer Maria Rilke, "And now we welcome the new year, full of things that have never been." Each moment is an invitation to reinvent ourselves, to embrace the unknown, and to create something extraordinary. The journey is yours to take—may it be one of growth, courage, and endless possibility.

ACKNOWLEDGEMENT

Creating this book has been a journey of exploration, growth, and collaboration, and it would not have been possible without the support and inspiration of many incredible individuals.

To my family and friends, your unwavering encouragement and belief in me have been the foundation upon which I've built this work. Thank you for your patience, love, and understanding as I immersed myself in this project.

To the thinkers, leaders, and innovators whose stories and insights fill these pages, thank you for the wisdom and inspiration you have shared with the world. Your journeys have illuminated the path of reinvention and have profoundly shaped my understanding of resilience and growth.

A heartfelt thanks to my editorial team and collaborators, whose expertise and dedication helped bring this vision to life. Your attention to detail and thoughtful guidance ensured that this book would resonate with readers as I had hoped.

Finally, to you, the reader, thank you for joining me on this journey. Your curiosity, openness, and commitment to growth are what make this work meaningful. I am grateful for the opportunity to share these ideas with you.

With deepest gratitude,
Felix Grayson

ABOUT THE AUTHOR

 Felix Grayson's journey into timeless wisdom began in child-hood, captivated by the stories of philosophers, leaders, and visionaries who shaped the way we think and live. Growing up in a home filled with books, he spent countless hours exploring ideas that asked life's biggest questions—a curiosity that would later define his work.

After facing his own modern challenges—balancing ambition, uncertainty, and the search for meaning - Felix discovered that the wisdom of the past offers profound guidance for the present. This realization became the foundation for the *Stoned Philosopher* series: a collection dedicated to translating ancient insights into practical lessons for today's world.

Felix's writing is more than reflection—it's an invitation to dialogue with history's greatest minds. Through each book, he helps readers find clarity, resilience, and purpose in their own lives—one timeless idea at a time.

When not writing, Felix enjoys quiet contemplation, deep conversation, and exploring the endless pursuit of wisdom in everyday moments.

www.ingramcontent.com/pod-product-compliance
Lightning Source LLC
Chambersburg PA
CBHW021223130626
46554CB00004B/1339